Leslie's Illustrated Civil War

LESLIE'S ILLUSTRATED

CIVIL WAR

With an Introduction by John E. Stanchak

UNIVERSITY PRESS OF MISSISSIPPI JACKSON & LONDON

The University Press of Mississippi
acknowledges with grateful appreciation the generosity of
Mrs. Fannie Kate Catchings of Woodville, Mississippi,
for allowing the use of her copy of
The Soldier in Our Civil War,
from which this facsimile edition was printed.

Printed in Singapore through Palace Press

95 94 93 92 4 3 2 1
The paper in this book meets the guidelines for permanence
and durability of the Committee on Production Guidelines for
Book Longevity of the Council on Library Resources.

Library of Congress Cataloging-in-Publication Data

Stanchak, John E.
    Leslie's Illustrated Civil War / with an introduction by John E.
    Stanchak.
        p.   cm.
    ISBN 0-87805-567-3 (alk. paper)
    1. United States–History–Civil War, 1861-1865–Pictorial works.
    I. Leslie, Frank, 1821-1880. Illustrated Civil War. II. Title.
    E468.7.S77 1992
    973.7–dc20   92-8815
                                                            CIP

British Library Cataloging-in-Publication data available

INTRODUCTION *by John E. Stanchak*

Like all enduring concepts, it was simple. In early 1862, a year which found the old Union dashed in two and the U.S. Government in tatters, New York City publishing entrepreneur Frank Leslie produced his *Pictorial History of the American Civil War.* The Northern public, impressed with the gravity of the nine-month-old conflict and hungry for explanations, bought the book in huge numbers, and Leslie turned a handsome profit. To the man or woman who could afford the outsized hardback volume, it did not matter that the Civil War was still going on and there was no end in sight. People wanted someone to make some sense of the confusing events of the day. Leslie, publisher of the popular national newsweekly *Frank Leslie's Illustrated Newspaper,* grasped this need and was eager to oblige.

In the months and years ahead other publications such as the *Richmond Examiner* and *Harper's Weekly* would produce their own mid-war "histories." Decades later publications such as *Time, Newsweek,* and *Life* would institutionalize the format, cranking out "year-end reviews" and thin histories of earth-shaking events. And in the late twentieth century television news organizations would take the concept a step further, producing late-night news analysis programs and video histories of wars, public scandals, and the downfalls of governments.

The concept Frank Leslie seized upon in 1862, using graphics and terse prose to interpret on-going news events, is still with us. And so is the product that followed it–the retrospective. Americans born after World War I have had their taste for history and nostalgia satisfied by books commemorating every event from the Stock Market Crash of 1929 to the mammoth rock music festival at Woodstock, New York, in 1969. Most recently, in recognition of the fiftieth anniversary of Pearl Harbor, scores of books and magazine retrospectives have recounted the December 1941 Japanese attack that dragged the country into World War II.

The book, *The Soldier in Our Civil War,* is progenitor of them all. Made up of woodcut engravings taken from issues of *Frank Leslie's Illustrated Newspaper* published between 1861 and 1865 and abridged text taken from other earlier Leslie's publications, it is not so much a history of the war as it is a nostalgic work, which reminded Union veterans or the widows and grown children of veterans what *their* war had been about. The present facsimile one-volume edition of *The Soldier in Our Civil War* is a copy of the original published in 1894, a year that saw a surge in public interest in what had come to be called "The Late Unpleasantness." It was the thirtieth anniversary of Confederate General Robert E. Lee's struggles with Union Lieutenant General U.S. Grant in

Virginia at Spotsylvania, the Wilderness, Cold Harbor, and in front of Petersburg. That year Americans also observed the thirtieth anniversary of Confederate General John Bell Hood's defeats at the Tennessee Battles of Franklin and Nashville, the capture and burning of Atlanta, Georgia, and Union Major General William T. Sherman's "March to the Sea."

A two-volume edition of *The Soldier in Our Civil War* had been published in 1891 and 1892, 30 years after the collapse of Fort Sumter or the Battle of Antietam. And prior to that, the old Leslie organization produced a large format two-volume work titled *Frank Leslie's Illustrated History of the Civil War.* Other similar volumes appeared at regular intervals dating back to the end of the war when the published work was a review of events and an extended exercise in exalting the Union victory.

The text for *The Soldier in Our Civil War* and its earlier incarnations was revised and rewritten often, but the illustrations for all these books had been reproduced from regular weekly editions of *Frank Leslie's Illustrated Newspaper* published during the war years. They were woodcut engravings made from sketches produced by battlefield artists employed by the Leslie organization–men who followed the contending Civil War armies and, in the age before the advent of newspaper photography, made a visual record of the action as it happened. Consequently, whether you are examining this reprint of *The Soldier in Our Civil War* or looking at remaining copies of *Frank Leslie's Illustrated Newspaper* from the war years, the scenes arrayed on the pages before you are those observed by Leslie's artists. By reproducing them for the first time in decades, the University Press of Mississippi is preserving an eyewitness account of the war's military adventures, and it is saving a visual history of the war in the field.

Is *The Soldier in Our Civil War* a complete visual history? No one survives who could argue the point with absolute authority. According to J. Cutler Andrews in his 1955 history of Union journalists, *The North Reports the Civil War*, "A few months before the end of the war, *Frank Leslie's* boasted that during the last four years at least one of its 'trained corps of the first artists' had accompanied every important expedition 'either by sea or land' and that it had published nearly three thousand pictures of 'battles, sieges, bombardments, stormings and other scenes, incidental to war,' contributed by more than eighty artists." We also know, however, from letters and memoirs by Leslie's artists, that the artists were often left behind by the armies, driven from the camps by unhappy generals, and occasionally confused about a troop's true position or the correct names of a locality. In addition, their drawings were sometimes edited by the wood engravers or their supervisors in New York who found it convenient to "clean up" the scenery–removing depictions of mutilated corpses or altering scenes to show "fighting generals" on the field in full-dress uniforms.

The obvious result is that if not a complete visual history of the Civil War, the old *Leslie's*[1] engravings make up a very wide-ranging record of the war years. From illustrations showing the April 1861 bombardment of Union-held Fort Sumter in South Carolina's Charleston Harbor to others depicting the 1864 naval battle between the Confederate raider *Alabama* and the USS *Kearsarge* off Cherbourg, France, they depict the technical and geographic means Americans undertook to settle their great domestic wrangle. By showing the record number of combat dead on the battlefield at Antietam in 1862 and the ragged and homeless

runaway slaves blindly following Sherman's men as they marched through the Carolinas in 1864, the engravings memorialize the depth of the struggle for the American people.

This reprint of *The Soldier in Our Civil War* preserves much of the record of the war. It tells us little, however, about the illustrated newspaper that first preserved that record, the artists who risked their lives to make it, or the publisher who risked his fortune to compile it. And, it tells us almost nothing about the men and women who gained fame and influence or who lost everything waging the war this book commemorates.

On the eve of the Civil War, the United States of America was a country that loved its newspapers. Whether they were read beneath a gas lamp in a fine Boston home or by the light of a candle in a crude Smokey Mountain cabin, newspapers were enjoyed for the stories of far-away places and events they carried, for the advertisements they displayed that brought the world of commerce to everyone's door, and for the rough jokes and columns of folksy wisdom they contained. They were also appreciated for the debate they generated.

In 1860 and 1861, America was a more complex country than it had ever been, and its newspapers reflected that fact. Though still dominated by white Anglo-Saxon Protestants, the U.S. was quickly becoming a nation with a diverse population: Irish and German Catholics, German Jews, people from central and southern Europe, and adventurers from every part of the globe kept steadily immigrating to North America. The Whig and Democratic parties, long the strongest influences in national politics, were being challenged, defeated and (in the case of the Whigs) obliterated by

a new force: the Republican party. The morality, profitability, and practicality of chattel slavery–the practice of holding Negro men, women, and children in lifetime bondage–a legal and accepted institution in roughly one-half the settled portion of the nation, was being challenged and repudiated in the halls of the U.S. Senate and House of Representatives, and in Northern and Southern drawing rooms and churches, and in national publications. These changes in the ethnic and political make-up of the United States helped turn debating into a national pastime in the early 1860s. Abetting the arguments was a strong, steady rise in the level of public literacy. South Carolina's Charleston *Mercury*, New York's Brooklyn *Eagle*, and Missouri's St. Louis *Evening News*–each then influential regional newspapers–discovered their circulation swelling each month. And *Frank Leslie's Illustrated Newspaper*, one of the handful of newspapers that could honestly call themselves "national," stood proud beside them. In the days before the bombardment of Fort Sumter ushered in the Civil War, *Leslie's* happily claimed circulation in excess of 100,000, North and South.

In those times when journalistic objectivity was an unknown ideal, when almost every news organ of any size held to a firm political point of view or was even owned outright by a political party or individual politician, and when expressed Union loyalty or avowed secessionist fervor was expected from editorial columns, *Frank Leslie's Illustrated Newspaper* stood apart. Except for tolerating anti-Irish sentiment and lampoons of African-Americans in its humor columns and favoring public health, Godliness, and the work ethic, *Leslie's* advocated or condoned little that was political. Like modern newspapers and news periodicals, its first and unabashed principle and goal was to turn a profit.

Publisher Frank Leslie himself had little interest in the growing sectional controversy in the late antebellum period. Embracing an early vision of what would one day be called the American Dream, he immigrated from Great Britain in 1848 determined to become a success. Leslie was christened

Henry Carter. Born in Ipswich on March 29, 1821, he demonstrated an early talent for wood engraving. In 1842, British journalist Herbert Ingram decided to take a gamble on improved printing techniques, launched the *Illustrated London News*, the first graphic newspaper, and hired young Carter as one of his engravers. The craft Carter learned in the Ingram organization was highly regarded and demanding. Ingram employed sketch artists to whom he would assign the task of attending public events and rendering pencil drawings of them. He then turned over these sketches to his engravers. Each engraver would take a sketch, attach it to a woodblock, trace the original image onto the block, then engrave it into the wood. The entire process, from the time the artist sketched the scene to the time it appeared in the *London Illustrated News* took approximately a month.

Carter signed all his *London Illustrated News* work with the pseudonym "Frank Leslie." After six years, he took his talent and pen name to America and signed on with famed U.S. showman P.T. Barnum, producing an illustrated catalog for Barnum's American Museum in New York City. From that position, he went on to one as an engraver for an early American illustrated magazine *Gleason's Pictorial.* Then in 1852, Barnum and a pair of investors launched their own version of Herbert Ingram's London product. Simply dubbed the *Illustrated News*, Barnum produced it for just a year before selling out all holdings to Gleason's and ceasing publication.

When Barnum launched his short-lived *Illustrated News*, he hired Carter-Leslie as engraving supervisor or chief foreman, according to several sources. During this period, the English engraver is believed to have originated the idea of taking a sketch, tracing the image on to a block of boxwood, and then cutting up the block into several pieces, each piece to be given to a separate engraver, preferably with some specialty–portraits, woodland scenery, horses, architecture or such. When all the engravers were finished, the pieces of the block were reassembled with a series of interlocking bolts, an

electroplate copy was made of the reconstructed wood engraving, and the electroplate piece sent to the printing plant.[2] The result of this technique of dividing the labor is that a public event could go from sketch to engraving to printed product within ten days to two weeks instead of the routine three to four weeks.

Carter-Leslie kept the new technique to himself during his time with Barnum. In 1853 he set up his own organization, and in January 1854 published the first issue of *Frank Leslie's Ladies' Gazette of Paris, London, and New York Fashions*, one of the first illustrated American fashion magazines. The immediate success and popularity of this magazine encouraged him to take the next, boldest step. In December 1855 he premiered the first issue of *Frank Leslie's Illustrated Newspaper*, his own light news publication using the multiple-engraver method. The result again was immediate public acceptance and a clamor for more coverage. Within four years, two competitive graphic newsweeklies, *Harper's Weekly* and the *New York Illustrated News* were launched and American readers sat back to enjoy the fruits of the competition that would determine the preeminent illustrated newsweekly in the nation.

In 1857 Henry Carter disappeared permanently. The British-born engraver legally changed his name to Frank Leslie and set out to build one of the top five publishing empires in mid-nineteenth century America. The supporting pillar of his organization was his *Illustrated Newspaper*. Because it had been the first graphic newsweekly, Leslie had an advantage over the other publications arriving on the scene. By accepting national advertising for products such as Steinway

pianos, Ward shirts, and Wheeler & Wilson sewing machines, the newspaper generated enough cash for Leslie to compete with other publishers for the services of America's small number of commercial artists.

Leslie directed the efforts of 130 engravers and printing artisans in the late 1850s from a five-story building at 19 City Hall Square in New York City. He recruited sketch artists from around the country and for publication often adapted the work of mildly-talented individuals who happened to witness newsmaking events. Racing beside him in the quest for talent was Fletcher Harper, a partner in the well-financed Harper & Brothers publishing house and himself publisher of Leslie's chief rival *Harper's Weekly*, the illustrated "Journal of Civilization." Harper incessantly connived to cajole artists into his employ and aggressively tried to beat Leslie's national distribution figures. The result was that by the start of the Civil War in April 1861 Leslie was only 10,000 readers ahead of Harper, and each had the services of one of the two best news sketch artists working in America, the British-born Waud brothers, William and Alfred. William Waud, the younger of the two, worked for Leslie. Suave and cynical, William ingratiated himself to members of polite society in Charleston, South Carolina, during the winter of 1860-61, the time of the "secession crisis."

A vote by state delegates in Charleston on December 20, 1860, took South Carolina out of the Union. State officials abruptly took possession of all federal property they could get. Within days of the vote to secede, U.S. Army Major Robert Anderson pulled all his personnel from defenses along the rim of Charleston Harbor and barracked them inside Fort Sumter, a red brick bastion situated on an island within artillery range of the city's waterfront. Determined to protect that piece of U.S. real estate, he sent word into the city that he did not seek a fight but he would defend his fort unless Washington officials instructed him to do otherwise. This circumstance positioned the Carolinians and the U.S. Army for war.

War would not break out for nearly three months. Charleston, a city awash with journalists and news artists from the North and South and abroad, held few strangers above suspicion. In this tense atmosphere, reporters and artists for most "Yankee" publications found they could not secure interviews and sittings. *Leslie's* young Waud, however, with his English accent and continental manners, gained entrance to Rebel gun emplacements and fortifications and Charleston dining rooms. He freely sketched portraits of South Carolina's Governor Pickens, his wife, family and entourage, along with the positions and make up of the imposing Southern harbor-side batteries and panoramas of enthusiastic pro-secession street demonstrations. Wherever he traveled, sketching news events, individuals were cooperative: Waud's foreign citizenship and the Leslie news organization's uncommitted editorial stance seemed to encourage them to explain the secessionist viewpoint. This artist's warm reception reaped benefits for *Frank Leslie's Illustrated Newspaper*. Its circulation kept a firm edge over *Harper's Weekly* during these early months as readers discovered William Waud was one of the few trained artists able to bring them the story of the crisis as it unfolded.

William Waud and *Leslie's* were both fortunate. Following Abraham Lincoln's November 1860 U.S. presidential election and the serious pursuit of secession on the part of most Southern states, several Northern papers printed appeasing editorials, offering new compromise proposals to preserve the nation or urging that the South be allowed to leave the Union in peace. In his book *Editors Make War* (1966), historian Donald E. Reynolds notes, however, that Southerners paid little attention to those moderate voices: "Although such newspapers were in the minority of Northern sheets, the Southern press chose to accentuate the negative opinions, rather than the more numerous positive ones. 'The tone of the Northern press, rostrum and pulpit,' said a formerly moderate Georgia paper, 'should convince all Southern men that the hour for dissolution is come and that

it is as inevitable as the fulfillment of the decrees of God.'"

Waud's employer perceived these secessionist sensitivities. As news historian W. Fletcher Thompson, Jr., wrote in his book *Images of War*, "Leslie instructed him to use the greatest discretion in making his sketches and to avoid giving the impression of being a Northern investigator. If necessary, he was to err in favor of the Carolinians." His advice worked well. Until the shooting started, *Leslie's* pictures helped the paper maintain an advantage over competitors. Waud was able to keep Northern readers and an ever-shrinking Southern subscribership on the edge of their setees with scenes of angry secessionists calling for a fight and with pictures of Union troops on Fort Sumter's parapets preparing to defend their lives and their flag. Then, in the days just before Confederate Brigadier General P.G.T. Beauregard ordered the firing of the first shot from Charleston, Waud received help.

Eugene Benson was a talented art student eager for a break. After executing a few simple jobs for *Leslie's*, Benson was hired full-time and sent to South Carolina to position himself for the coming fight. The editorial plan was, that when the shooting started, both Benson and Waud would sketch the action from as many vantage points as possible. At 4:30 on the morning of April 12, 1861, the Confederate batteries ringing Charleston Harbor opened fire on Sumter. The fight lasted until near 1:00 P.M., April 14. Throughout the entire battle Waud and Benson prowled the harborside, sketching furiously. Both men were certain that what they had in hand could not be bested by any other news organization. They faced only one last hurdle; how to get their sketches to New York?

In the last days before the fight, President Abraham Lincoln dispatched a naval expedition to see if it would be possible to resupply Fort Sumter. Among the ships sent were the *Baltic*, *Pocahontas*, and *Harriet Lane*. Unfortunately for the Union cause, in the end the only chore left to these vessels was to transport Major Anderson and his surrendered

garrison north to New York City. In the best competitive traditions of old-fashioned journalism, Waud and Benson tried to convince an officer of the *Baltic* he should take their work to the *Leslie's* offices in City Hall Square once he had delivered his cargo of battered Union heroes. They hinted that if the officer had made any sketches himself, Mr. Leslie might be inclined to publish them. Waud and Benson came close to persuading the man, but in the end he suspected bribery and declined. Meanwhile, a New York *World* reporter named B.S. Osbon ingratiated himself to Major Anderson and secured a ride north with the fleet. When he arrived in New York, Osbon, not a trained artist, sold some of his own sketches to publications and beat the *Leslie's* men on their scoop. (Some pictures of the Fort Sumter bombardment had appeared before Osbon's, but they were based on written descriptions, not sketches by eyewitnesses.)

Benson made a few last sketches depicting Sumter as a charred and shattered wreck. Two days after Anderson had departed with the fleet, he found transportation north, taking with him his own and Waud's drawings. In New York he discovered the *Leslie's* offices in the grip of patriotic fever. The attack on Sumter had knocked publisher Leslie off his position on the political fence and into an alliance with the Union camp. Eager to stoke the patriotic fire, Leslie dispatched artists to all parts of the North and western border states to capture the public's mood and, in places such as Kentucky and Missouri, to record the ongoing and fearsome debate over secession.

Leslie's "special artists," or "specials" as they were known to journalists, covered anti-Union riots in St. Louis and Baltimore, recruiting drives in Chicago, Louisville and Boston, and wild parades in New York City and other metropolitan areas, where militia regiments departing for the South brandished knives or bayonets and posed for press sketches. The consummate entrepreneur, Leslie realized his current staff would never meet the Civil War's demand for graphics. Thompson explained how Leslie addressed the need: "Leslie solicited sketches from officers and soldiers alike, and he offered a year's free subscription to anyone in the service who submitted a small sketch as a sample of his ability as an artist. Whenever regiments passed through New York, he asked any volunteer who could sketch to call on him at his office." Leslie then went on a recruiting drive for trained artists. This effort won him the services of some of the best, aspiring sketchmen in the North.

One of Leslie's finest discoveries was Arthur Lumley. A student at the National Academy of Design who had worked for Leslie part-time, Lumley impressed the publisher with his sketches of the farewell parade of then-Colonel Ambrose Burnside's regiment in Providence, Rhode Island. He was hired full-time and assigned to follow the career of the army being built up around Washington, D.C., in late spring 1861. Another of Leslie's talented "specials" was Henri Lovie, a lithographer from Cincinnati and before the war, an occasional contributor to *Frank Leslie's Illustrated Newspaper*. He became a full-time staff member, first assigned to cover Lincoln's first days in Washington and then sent into western Virginia to follow the fortunes of a then little-known brigadier general named George B. McClellan. Artist C.S. Hall, a long-time professional, was taken on to cover the secessionist disturbances in Baltimore, Maryland, and then later assigned to cover the Federal army in Virginia. Francis "Frank" H. Schell of Philadelphia was also hired to follow military developments in Virginia. William Waud, now the darling of the offices on City Hall Square, was sent roving wherever the news seemed the hottest.

In the months and years ahead some of these artists would depart and be replaced by talents such as James E. Taylor–a detail-oriented sketchman who spent the first two years of the Civil War as a Union private and later, for *Leslie's*, made a graphic record of Union Major General Philip Sheridan's 1864 campaigns in Virginia's Shenandoah Valley. Philadelphian Frederick B. Schell, a kinsman of Frank Schell, covered the 1863 Vicksburg Campaign. Edwin Forbes joined the Leslie organization in early 1862 after studying at the National Academy of Design and working as an apprentice under a craftsman who specialized in making prints of horse races and thoroughbreds. He was assigned to cover the Union's Army of the Potomac and stayed with it until late 1864. Of all Frank Leslie's troop of sketch artists, Forbes would, over the course of a long lifetime, prove the most prolific, turning his war-era experiences into a decades-long career.

William Waud, Eugene Benson, the Schells, Lovie and the others were the graphic reporters who informed *Leslie's* subscribers and created the body of work that would one day fill Frank Leslie's compendia of Civil War material, including this facsimile. And they may have been among the war's most invisible group of heroes.

The Civil War was the adventure of their lives. Moving from one war theater to another, the men of Frank Leslie's corps of artists were routinely exposed to hostile gunfire, foul weather, disease, and the possibility of capture. They were also exposed to opportunities that, but for the unusual condition of the nation, otherwise might never have come their way. Through their assignments, a number of them met Abraham Lincoln, famous generals and statesmen and well-known actors and celebrities. *Leslie* artist Arthur Lumley even had the opportunity to experience life on the technological edge, riding in an observation balloon piloted by the celebrated nineteenth-century aeronaut Thaddeaus Lowe. Lumley's 1862 sketches made from Lowe's balloon *Intrepid* make up some of the most breathtaking panoramas executed during the war years. His drawings of the craft, aloft, being towed from below by a Union navy vessel on Virginia's James River, make him perhaps the first man ever to produce a picture of an aircraft carrier.

Unusual escapades such as Lumley's were definitely not routine for Leslie's artists. Escaping a "close call" on the battlefield, however, was a common occurrence. Henri Lovie was one of Frank Leslie's most productive artists in the war's first years. Noted for sketching very rapidly, he would ride almost anywhere on a battlefield and produce volumes of work from which Frank Leslie and his editors selected the best. But his penchant for almost intrusive activity nearly cost him his life. Lovie had been present for the brief Battle of Phillipi in western Virginia on June 3, 1861, by later standards not much more than an outsized skirmish. The "battle" was fought by green farm boys and mercantile clerks in uniform, new volunteers with virtually no combat experience. The scrape left the new soldiers nervous, and even after the opposing armies withdrew, they remained alert for some new movement by the enemy.

A few days after the affair Lovie was reconnoitering the area on horseback with some Union officers when nervous Yankee pickets mistook them for Confederate scouts. A bullet whistled over Lovie's head and he rode for cover, a move that brought on a heavy rain of gunfire. Finally, through persistent shouting, the artist convinced them he was a Northern newsman. More angry than frightened, Lovie returned to camp where he told a fellow journalist from Cincinnati that, although he did not object to running reasonable risks from the enemy, "it would be damnably unpleasant to be killed by mistake."

Lovie is a significant and fascinating figure in Civil War journalism. He traveled widely, especially in the western theater. Within several months he covered the Battle of Lexington, Missouri, the fall of Forts Henry and Donelson in Tennessee, the capture of Island Number 10 on the Mississippi River near New Madrid, Missouri, and the campaign that culminated in the April 1862 Battle of Shiloh.

He wrote often to his employer and to his large family. His correspondence records experiences in Missouri where in 1861 he became a member of a group of journalists who called themselves the "Bohemian Brigade." These hard-drinking jokers were just as likely to organize horse races, vandalize boarding houses, and carry out impetuous pranks as to follow the army into battle.

Lovie's correspondence regarding Shiloh is almost as telling as his pictures of it that won this praise from a contemporary: "No other artist in the war illustrated a battle as well as Henri Lovie sketched the battle of Shiloh." Lovie wrote to Leslie, describing the last victorious Union charge on the second and last day of this fight in Tennessee. "The scene was a fearful one. Our artillerists worked with the utmost rapidity, branches torn by the enemy's shots, who fortunately fired too high, flying in every direction; shot and shell rushing through the timber, while the road close by was covered with an inextricable confusion of wagons, ambulances, wounded, stragglers, mules, and horses, struggling to gain the transports on the river." Then, a few days later, he again wrote Leslie, this time that he was a casualty of the campaign. Louis M. Starr, author of *Bohemian Brigade,* quoted Lovie's letter in his account of the lives of Civil War field correspondents:

"Riding from 10 to 15 miles daily, through mud and underbrush, and then working until midnight by the dim light of an attenuated tallow 'dip,' are among the least of my desagremens and sorrows. . . . I am nearly 'played out' and as soon as Pittsburgh [Landing] is worked up, and Corinth settled, I must beg a furlough for rest and repairs. I am deranged about the stomach, ragged, unkempt and unshorn, and need the co-joined skill and services of the apothecary, the tailor and the barber, and above all the attentions of home . . . ."

Lovie got his break. In Mississippi covering U.S. Grant's campaign to take Vicksburg, he invested in a cotton buying scheme and quickly and unexpectedly became modestly wealthy. The money freed him of the necessity of tramping through malarial climates and ducking enemy artillery rounds. He quit the Leslie organization and went home to Cincinnati, never to sketch again. In the end, only through reprints such as *The Soldier in Our Civil War* would his work be preserved.

When the combat experiences of all the Leslie artists are taken into account, perhaps few exceed those of James E. Taylor, an Ohio native. His pre-war art education was paid for by wealthy patron Nicholas Longworth, but following the outbreak of hostilities he left his studies in New York City and joined the 10th New York Volunteer Infantry. Taylor's service took him to the Virginia peninsula, south of Richmond. There he began contributing to *Leslie's* as a freelance artist. On the expiration of his enlistment, he joined the *Leslie's* staff full-time and took the assignment of following Major General Philip Sheridan's army in the Shenandoah Valley in the autumn of 1864. Then, he began a unique project. He made duplicates of sketches he submitted to the New York office and saved them for a time in later life when he could fill them out and convert them to watercolors, wash drawings, or simply more fulsome pen and ink works. Along with these works he kept a journal. Today in the possession of the Western Reserve Historical Society, his journal and the accompanying sketches preserve a record of some scenes that never got into *Leslie's*–Union surgeons at their grisly work in a church, and Union soldiers robbing a blinded Confederate officer–and others that did and made a lasting impression on the public.

One scene Taylor recorded was the climax of "Sheridan's Ride." On October 19, 1864, the Union commander galloped miles from the town of Winchester to rally his army under surprise attack from Confederate Lieutenant General Jubal Early's troops at Cedar Creek. Sheridan passed through streams of retreating men calling out "Forward Boys! Follow me!" then, mounted on his warhorse Rienzi and carrying the flag, led them in a crushing counterattack. This incident in history inspired a popular patriotic poem and several fine paintings. But Taylor had the privilege of recording it first and *Frank Leslie's Illustrated Newspaper* of publishing it first. Generations of readers looked forward to Taylor's sketches in Leslie's Civil War books.

Other moving incidents that Taylor recorded and Leslie published are not as well-remembered. Among them was the death of Confederate Major General Stephen D. Ramseur. This Southern officer, the youngest officer of his grade in the Army of Northern Virginia, was a well-liked graduate of the West Point class of 1860. Many of his friends served opposite him in Sheridan's army, Brigadier General George Armstrong Custer among them. In the Cedar Creek fight Ramseur was mortally wounded and taken to a nearby mansion, Belle Grove, to die in peace, comforted by his old classmates. Taylor visited the mansion the following day. "The Generals Hd Qts were in front of the mansion," Taylor wrote in his journal:

"While between me and the tents was parked 45 captured guns, 24 being recovered Union guns taken from us in the morning surprise, and to the left of the tents were 1,000 graybacks under guard destined for Northern prisons besides Army wagons and Ambulances, all part of the spoils of the Victory. It was a refreshing sight. The gratifying subject transferred to my pad I approach the mansion to view the remains of General Ramseur who expired from his wounds during the night.

Entering the building I am directed by the guard to the north east room; the guests chamber, with oak panelling over the fire place. . . . Once within I uncover [removes his hat] in presence of the dead.

With the body was a Confederate surgeon and Generals Aide, Major Hutchinson, who with tender touch were dressing the remains for the grave. Calm and peaceful lay the Noble Browed Soldier–of Majestic Mein who clothed in a handsome uniform, with gauntleted hand over breast, emblematic of rest and sword at side, presented a picture, even in death, of the ideal Warrior. Twas with difficulty my pencil performed its offices, so affected was I by the stern repose of the features."

This scene sketched by Taylor, his depiction of Sheridan's timely arrival at Cedar Creek, Lovie's Shiloh battle sketches and many more scenes preserved by his colleagues appeared in *Leslie's* and *The Soldier in Our Civil War* and ended up being more than a depiction of history in the making. They became history themselves. But the majority of the artists, their names and reputations, and pictures have almost faded from the historical record. A brief discussion of publishing in Frank Leslie's time helps explain why.

William Waud, the most technically competent of all the artists in Frank Leslie's stable, quit *Leslie's* in mid-1863 and went to work for *Harper's Weekly*. In 1862 *Harper's Weekly* hired William's brother Alfred away from the *New York Illustrated News*. The *News'* publisher, T. B. Leggett, trying to stay ahead of the game, raided Leslie's staff and hired away Arthur Lumley. Other artists came and went as the war dragged on.

Frank Leslie's "specials" were paid only when their sketches were published. A larger news event might push one man's work out for another's. When F. C. Bonwill, *Leslie's* artist following Union Major General Nathaniel Banks' 1864 Red River Expedition through Louisiana, lost months of work to enemy capture, he went unpaid. The same thing happened to Leslie "special" Joseph Becker along Virginia's Rappahannock River. Sometimes, Mr. Leslie was simply whimsical about what he did with his money. At one point shortly before the Civil War, his engravers complained about

going unpaid for three weeks. His accountant blithely explained to them that Mr. Leslie had purchased a yacht and needed the capital.

If poor and erratic pay led to a lack of artist loyalty, the absence of any benefits for those pursuing a hazardous occupation certainly did nothing to improve it. As Confederate General Robert E. Lee's men marched north toward Gettysburg, Pennsylvania, in summer 1863, they captured two *Leslie's* artists, George Law and C. E. F. Hillen. Both were later released, then Hillen joined Sherman's campaign on Atlanta in spring 1864 and was badly wounded. Henry Lovie was once threatened with lynching by Confederate sympathizers in Kentucky. A *Leslie's* part-time artist named James O'Neill was killed in combat. Many were often ill and away from work and pay because of fevers contracted in the field. So, regardless of what work-related trouble befell them, the artists and their families were left wanting.

In addition to losing artists, by mid-war *Leslie's* was losing strength and influence. Shortly after the twin Confederate defeats at Gettysburg and Vicksburg in July 1863, events that filled *Leslie's* with dramatic illustrations, and events that should have pushed the number of *Leslie's* readers to new highs, helped *Harper's Weekly* to surge ahead in distribution. For the first time in its short history *Leslie's* surrendered the lead in its circulation war with *Harper's* and the *New York Illustrated News*.

Frank Leslie himself, it is reported, attributed his problems to the loss of good artists. He was, in fact, partially correct: the work done for competitors by William Waud's brother Alfred and *Harper's* artist Theodore Davis was superior to most of the material appearing in *Leslie's* at that time. But many historians, looking deeper, also see errors in Frank Leslie's ability to gauge the public temperament and the political climate.

Just prior to the outbreak of the Civil War, Leslie made a conscious editorial decision to give offense to no political viewpoint, hoping that if war were averted he would not

have alienated his Southern subscribers. Then, following the attack on Fort Sumter and the loss of his Southern readership, he embraced hopes for Union victory. Perhaps being more astute as a newspaper and magazine salesman than as an observer of the American scene, Leslie did not mature politically beyond that point, and his newspaper suffered as a result.

As the ongoing war bred issues more complex than simply winning the contest and preserving the Union, the publisher and his paper fell behind. For instance, though a vocal minority protested the institution of a national military draft, a serious majority favored it and saw it as essential to winning the war for the Union. Ernest A. McKay noted in his recent history *The Civil War and New York City* (1990) that *Leslie's* declared that the draft transformed the republic into "one grand military dictatorship." McKay also noted that later, when many whites slowly came to see the emancipation of the slaves as a necessary step in prosecuting the war against the South, the immigrant publisher continued to oppose it. He sympathized little with slaves, who he said were "sensual, gluttonous, thievish, and hopelessly lazy."

Though thoughtful Leslie's subscribers may have perceived the publisher as holding "politically incorrect" views, those who opposed the war or actively supported the Confederacy did not believe Mr. Leslie to be in their camp either. *Frank Leslie's Illustrated Newspaper* and other mainstream Northern publications were generally reviled by war opponents. And in the South, where badly worn dog-eared copies still managed to get across the battle lines and into Confederate homes, *Leslie's* was considered little more than a propaganda tool for the Lincoln Administration. A young woman from Georgia named Eliza Frances Andrews made this abundantly clear in her war-time journal:

August 18, 1865: "I hate the Yankees more and more, every time I look at one of their horrid newspapers and read the lies they tell about us, while we have our mouths closed and padlocked. The world will not hear our story, and we must figure just as our enemies choose to paint us. The pictures in 'Harper's Weekly' and 'Frank Leslie's' tell more lies than Satan himself was ever the father of. I get in such a rage when I look at them that I sometimes take off my slipper and beat the senseless paper with it."

With no sound political base and continuing difficulty in recruiting artists, some stories went uncovered and the status of *Frank Leslie's Illustrated Newspaper* suffered. For instance, a *Harper's* sketchman accompanied Sherman on his "March to the Sea," but Leslie did not have anyone to cover that assignment until the army tramped into Savannah on the sea. All *Leslie's* coverage of that phase of the war begins in coastal Georgia and follows Sherman's troops through South and North Carolina to the last fight in that theater, the March 1865 Battle of Bentonville. Instead of fighting Fletcher Harper's operation head on, Frank Leslie contented himself with second place. He pursued instead the business strategy modern entrepreneurs call diversification, feeding more money into smaller publications he had started over the few previous years and launching new ones. By 1864, in addition to his *Illustrated Newspaper*, he published *Frank Leslie's Illustrate Zeitung*, a German-language edition aimed at the North's expanding Germanic immigrant population, a joke and cheap fiction publication called *Frank Leslie's Budget of Fun, Frank Leslie's Ten Cent Monthly, Frank Leslie's Lady's Illustrated Almanac*, and *Frank Leslie's Lady's Magazine and Gazette of Fashion*. (Throughout his career, the only publication he launched that did not bear his name was *Day's Doings*.)

At the war's end, most of his combat artists left the field of illustration. The much-praised Henri Lovie who retired early, died shortly after the close of hostilities. Early wartime *Leslie's* favorites William Waud and Arthur Lumley still pursued careers as illustrators but never returned to the conflict as a subject for their work, and Frank Schell only briefly resurrected the experience when he was commissioned by *Century* magazine to do a series of sketches for its long-running "Battles and Leaders" articles. Of all the newspaper's

wartime alumni, only Edwin Forbes, observer of the Army of Potomac, extended the *Leslie's* war legacy, producing collections of etchings entitled *Life Studies of the Great Army*, which were gold medal winners at the 1876 Centennial Exposition, and *Thirty Years After: An Artist's Story of the Great War*.

Harkening back to the success of his 1862 *Pictorial History of the American Civil War*, in postbellum days Frank Leslie began periodically to reissue the work of these men in his series of Civil War retrospectives and histories, often giving the artists credit in bold print on the title page, but, in those days before more comprehensive copyright arrangements, no more money. Then, in 1874 Leslie married Mirriam Folline, a writer and editor at his *Lady's Journal*. Several business reversals followed. At the time of his death, January 10, 1880, his enterprise was in receivership.

Mirriam Leslie (who would later marry critic William Wilde, brother of British literary figure Oscar), possessed great business acumen, engineered the financial rescue of the Leslie organization, kept up production of the Civil War books and other derivative material, and in 1882 changed *her* name to "Frank Leslie." In this later period, she sold reprint rights to many old Leslie titles. This facsimile of the reprint of *The Soldier in Our Civil War*, originally published in two volumes by her, is a case in point.

Reduced to a skeletal form, that is the story of this facsimile edition of *The Soldier in Our Civil War* and the people and the organization behind it. The reader of this book should remember that the original volume was popular in the states of the old victorious Union at a time when Southerners were

promoting the noble "Lost Cause" view of the conflict, wooing Yankee business investments, and enacting "Jim Crow" laws. It was parlor reading in an era when the Old West frontier was at last succumbing to the iron-handed civilizing influence of well-meaning Christian ladies and barbershop harmony was the coming musical craze. The first readers of this book took it off the shelf almost one hundred Memorial Days ago, when children were still begging fathers to "tell me again what you did in the war." And we should all keep in mind this one fact: within these covers, what is not art is artifact. This work is made up of pictures created in a time before cameras could capture motion; engraving was the only widely available medium that could capture and forever freeze the action that took place on America's most blood-soaked battlefields. What we see is what the artist saw.

In conclusion, those who question the truthfulness with which these pictures were rendered, either by the artists or old Mr. Leslie, may remember the Union's General Sherman. In autumn 1861, he expelled *Leslie's* artist Henry Lovie from his camp, saying, "I have steadily refused to admit reporters of any kind within my lines."

"But, General," Lovie pleaded, "I am no reporter or correspondent, not writing more than a brief description of my sketches."

"You fellows," snorted Sherman, "make the best paid spies that can be bought. Jeff Davis owes more to you newspaper men than to his army."

[1] The title *Leslie's*, used here and elsewhere in this introduction, refers to *Frank Leslie's Illustrated Newspaper*.

[2] The belief that Leslie was the sole inventor of this technique is disputed by some sources, who suggest evidence that the new process was a logical development in the evolution of an outmoded system.

THE SOLDIER

IN OUR

CIVIL WAR.

ABRIDGED EDITION.

Famous War Pictures

Illustrating the Valor of the Soldier as Displayed on the Battlefield. Sketched on the Spot by Famous War Artists.

NEW YORK:

STANLEY-BRADLEY PUBLISHING CO.

FAMOUS WAR PICTURES.

DURING the Civil War, Mr. Frank Leslie sent out about twenty skillful and world-renowned artists, one to be connected with each Department of the Army, with instructions to spare no expense in obtaining sketches of every battle, skirmish and military movement, to give to the anxious ones at home a vivid and realistic picture of the real war. These artists were selected from the masters of graphic delineation, and included such names as Forbes, Waud, Taylor, Becker, Lovie, Schell, Crane, Davis, etc. The sketches from their pencils drawn on the battle-field amid shot and shell, and inspired by the thrilling scenes and stirring times, are true to the battle life. These brave men went out with their respective army and navy corps, and took the unmerciful chances of war in the pursuit of their artistic, yet dangerous, but necessary calling. Their vivid delineation of a cavalry charge, the heroic and intrepid courage displayed by the rider, the eagerness of the noble steed as he dashed forward to face the combat, and finally the bursting of a treacherous shell, or a bullet from an unerring rifle, separating horse and rider forever, form an impressive and thrilling tableau, which gives us a most vigorous outline of the havoc and horrors of war, and these tableaux cannot be had in any other work in existence. Naval engagements, storming of fortifications, bombardments, bayonet charges, in fact, every battle fought and every incident of any importance recorded during the War, have been as faithfully sketched by the artists referred to, and appear as realistic to the old veteran who examines this great work, as if he were again standing on the field of action. The truthfulness of detail, force of character, accuracy of portraiture and depth of panoramic effect, carry us in imagination into the heart of the conflict, and make us as it were, close observers of the naval and military glory, so cleverly shown by the genius of the artist. The illustrations alone furnish a realistic view of war in a greater degree of comprehensiveness than hundreds of pages of text would be capable of supplying, and are invaluable as a supplement to every History of the Civil Conflict. The Veteran recognizes in the faces, action, situation, and standards, old and familiar friends, and with these pictures before him can tell his children " how the day was lost or won."

From these original War plates of Frank Leslie's Illustrated Newspaper from 1861-65 were selected the best engravings, rejecting all not absolutely pictorial and bearing on the truth of history, as proved by the participants on both sides, as well as the European authorities, published during the past twenty-five years, and they were re-touched at a cost of over $10,000. From these were produced " THE SOLDIER IN OUR CIVIL WAR " (for a description of which see third page of cover), the only authentic, Pictorial History in existence. This famous work has had probably the largest sale of any illustrated work in the United States, and it is from the original wood cuts used in making these plates that this abridged edition is printed. In this way we are enabled to furnish to every home a series of authentic and realistic War scenes at a mere nominal cost, which will supplement and help in the study of any History of the Civil War.

The publishers claim that never before in the annals of book-making has there been presented such a valuable and instructive collection of engravings for the home at so low a cost.

Entered according to Act of Congress, in the year one thousand eight hundred and ninety four, by
THE STANLEY BRADLEY PUBLISHING COMPANY,
In the Office of the Librarian of Congress, at Washington.

TABLE OF CONTENTS.

TABLE OF CONTENTS.—(*Continued.*)

BATTLE OF GETTYSBURG.—Charge of Pickett's brigade on Cemetery Hill, Thursday night, July 2, 1863.   The battle of Gettysburg, Pa., was fought on Wednesday, Thursday and Friday, July 1st, 2d and 3d, 1863.   The Federal army, 80,000 strong, was commanded by Major General Geo. F. Meade, and the Confederate forces of about equal strength were commanded by General Robert E. Lee.   The losses on the Federal side numbered 2,834 killed, 13,733 wounded and 6,643 missing.   The Confederates estimated their loss in killed, wounded and prisoners, at 36,000.   The result of the battle was the retreat of Lee's Army on the third day, when they recrossed the Potomac and marched down the Shenandoah valley toward Richmond.   The actual time of engagement was twenty-one hours.   From a sketch made on the battle field by A. Berghaus.

1

OCCUPATION OF BEAUFORT, S. C., December 5, 1861.—The brigade of General Isaac I. Stevens, taking possession of the city at night. The city is the capital of Beaufort county and is situated on Port Royal Island, and on an arm of the sea known as Port Royal River. Beaufort is a port of entry and has a good harbor with about sixteen feet of water over the bar. From a sketch made by W. T. Crane, who accompanied the army.

BATTLE OF CHICKAMAUGA, GA.—Repulse of the Confederate charge led by General Cleborne, at Crawfish Creek on the evening of the 19th. The battle of Chickamauga was fought on September 19th, 20th and 21st, 1863, between General W. S. Rosecrans, commanding the Federal army, comprised of 45,000 troops and the Confederate army 70,000 strong, commanded by General Braxton Bragg. The Federal losses were 1,644 killed, 9,262 wounded and 4,945 taken prisoners. The Confederates place their loss at 17.804 killed, wounded and prisoners. The Confederates captured 36 guns and 8,450 small arms, and were the victors. From a sketch made by J. F. E. Hillen.

3

THE FIRST BATTLE OF BULL RUN.—Advance of the Federal army on Sunday, July 21, 1861. This battle lasted for six hours. The Federal army of 35,000 men was commanded by General Irvin McDowell. The Confederate forces of equal strength were under the joint command of Generals Joseph E. Johnston and G. T. Beauregard. The losses of the Federal army were 481 killed, 1,011 wounded and 1460 missing. The Confederates lost in killed 267, wounded 1,483, prisoners 1,461. They captured 20 guns and 4,000 stand of arms. The Federal troops were routed and fell back to the fortifications around Washington, the victorious Confederates did not follow the retreating army. From a sketch by H. Lovie.

INVESTMENT OF FORTS JACKSON AND ST. PHILIP.—By Admiral Farragut's fleet, April 18, 1862. The "Fire Rafts" let loose from Fort Jackson to destroy the Federal fleet, intercepted and turned out of their course by the boats of the squadron, aided by the ferry-boat "Westfield." Fort Jackson was a bastioned fortification, built of brick with casements and glacis rising twenty-five feet above the water. Fort St. Philip was smaller and rose nineteen feet. They were mounted with 119 guns, mostly smooth-bore thirty-two pounders. Below the fort two iron chains were stretched across the river, supported by eight hulks anchored abreast. From a sketch by William Waud.

Duryee's Zouaves Skirmishing.   The Steuben Regiment's Assault—Col. Bendix.   Charge of Duryee's Zouaves.   Three-gun Battery, Lieutenant Greble.
Col. Townsend Deploying Two Companies to Act as Skirmishers.   Albany Regiment, Col. Townsend, in Line of Battle.   First New York, Col. Allen.   Second New York, Col. Carr.

THE FIRST BATTLE OF THE WAR.—Fought at Big Bethel, Virginia, June 10, 1861.   The Federal troops 3,000 strong, were commanded by Brigadier-general Pierce.   The Confederates had 1,800 men under General J. B. Magruder.   The battle lasted two-and-a-half hours, and the Federals lost 18 killed, 53 wounded and 5 missing.   The Confederates loss was, 8 killed, 20 wounded and 6 taken prisoners.   The victory was gained by the Confederates.   From a sketch by H. Lovie.

BATTLE OF CEDAR MOUNTAIN, August 9, 1862.—Confederate batteries shelling the Federal position at night. McDowell's corps marching to the field. This engagement lasted two hours. General John Pope commanded the Federal army at the time, and the forces engaged were the Second and Third army corps, under the immediate command of Generals Banks and McDowell, while General "Stonewall" Jackson directed the movements of the Confederates. The Federal loss was nearly 2,000 in killed, wounded and missing, besides a large quantity of arms and munitions of war. The Confederates loss was about 1,300. From a sketch by Edwin Forbes.

7

HILTON HEAD, PORT ROYAL HARBOR, S. C.—A view of the bombardment of the Confederate forts by the Federal fleet, November 7, 1861, sketched from the ramparts of Fort Walker during the bombardment by a confederate officer. The Federal fleet was comprised of fifteen vessels, commanded by Commodore S. F. Dupont. The Confederate forts "Walker" and "Beauregard" were splendidly garrisoned, and mounted 43 guns of heavy calibre, under the command of Commodore Tatnell. The forts were forced to surrender, and the Federal losses in the engagement were 8 killed, 23 wounded, while the Confederate loss, was about 100 killed, 100 wounded and 2,500 taken prisoners, with 42 guns. From a sketch by W. T. Crane.

ISLAND No. 10.—Night expedition by Colonel Roberts, with forty picked men of the Forty-second Illinois regiment, spiking the guns of the upper battery, April 1, 1862, during a violent hurricane. In the siege of Island No. 10, the Federal commanded by General John Pope, and the naval forces by Commodore A. H. Foote. The Confederate forces were commanded by General Beauregard. On April 6th, he determined to evacuate the island, and after sinking a steamboats, so as to obstruct the channel he turned over the command to General V. D. McCall, while with the main portion of his army he retired to Corinth. On April 7, 1862, the Island was surrendered to General Pope, including Generals McCall, Walker and Ganth, 123 guns and mortars, besides 10,000 stand of arms, a floating battery, several steamboats and a large quantity of ammunition and stores. From a sketch by Henry Lovie.

BATTLE OF SPOTTSYLVANIA COURT HOUSE, VA., May 8, 1864.—The battles of the Wilderness actually extended from May 5 to June 1, 1864, and the struggle for supremacy between General Grant, with 130,000 men of whom 100,000 were effective, and General Lee with 60,000 men, was stubbornly contested, and out of the struggle came the historic words of Grant, "I will fight it out on this line if it takes all Summer." The Battle of the Wilderness was really fought on June 5th and 6th, and the engagements thereafter took the names of the locations. In the first battle both armies had become thoroughly exhausted, and sought needed rest on the 7th. General Grant had some advantage, and followed it up on the evening of the 7th by advancing the Cavalry and Warren's Fifth corps towards Spottsylvania Court House. This movement was anticipated by General Lee, who withdrew his entire army, and had it entrenched behind breastworks at the Court House, on the evening of the 7th. In the Federal advance the Cavalry were repulsed, and Warren's corps came to their relief, and stubbornly fought their way until evening, when they had gained a favorable position in front of Longstreet's line. They were then reinforced by the Sixth corps, and made an unsuccessful assault on Longstreet, but were driven back and rested for the night and the next day. From a sketch by Edwin Forbes.

GENERAL GRANT AND HIS BODY-GUARD Crossing Mayfield Bridge in a reconoissance in force towards Columbus, Ky., to prevent the Confederates sending troops from that place to reinforce General Sterling Price, then advancing into Missouri. His short but energetic campaign had already attracted attention. September 1, 1861, he had been made a brigadier-general, and placed in command of the district of S. E. Missouri, with headquarters at Cairo. He seized Paducah on September 6th and thus saved Kentucky to the Union. In November he made a demonstration on Belmont and spent December and January (1862) in urging the War Department to join the land and naval forces in an expedition against Fort Henry. From a sketch by Henry Lovie.

11

RECONNOISSANCE By the Federal Cavalry in the neighborhood of Fairfax Court House, Va., previous to the first battle of Bull Run or Manassas. From a sketch by Edwin Forbes.

GALLANT CHARGE OF CUSTER'S CAVALRY In which they captured the guns of the Confederate forces under General J. E. B. Stuart near Culpepper, Va., September 14, 1863. The cavalry fight of this date lasted for four hours. The first second and third divisions of the Federal cavalry corps under command of General Kilpatrick, met the forces of Generals Lomas and Beale, composed of cavalry and artillery, with J. E. B. Stuart, the celebrated cavalry leader at their head. The losses were small on either side and the position was held by the Federal forces. From a sketch by Edwin Forbes.

BATTLE OF PITTSBURGH LANDING (SHILOH), Sunday, April 6, 1862.—General Grant with 32,000 men arrived at Pittsburgh Landing, April 1st, and had ordered General Buell to leave Nashville, and join him. While awaiting the arrival of Buell, General Albert S. Johnston with 45,000 Confederate troops made battle on the morning of the 6th, and forced Grant back to the river. The desperate defense made by General McClernand's division, composed of the 11th, 17th, 18th, 20th, 45th, 48th and 49th Illinois, the 8th Indiana and the 11th Iowa regiments, as they stood up before the terrible onslaught of Johnston and Beauregard, until the arrival of Buell in the afternoon, when the assault was repulsed, is the subject of the sketch by Henry Lovie.

GENERAL ROUSSEAU RECAPTURING HIS ARTILLERY At the battle of Pittsburgh Landing, Monday, April 7, 1862. On Sunday evening, April 6th, the Confederates lost their leader, General A. S. Johnston, who was mortally wounded and General Beauregard assumed command. On the morning of the 7th General Grant having received reinforcements from General Buell, which made his force equal to that of the Confederates, and support from the gunboats in the river. opened the battle with a heavy artillery fire, followed with a general assault which was resisted until the middle of the afternoon, when he recaptured his lines and cannon lost the previous day, and before dark drove the Confederates to hasty retreat. The Federal losses were 1,700 killed, 7,495 wounded, 3,022 prisoners, and the Confederates loss, 1,728 killed, 8,012 wounded and 959 missing. From a sketch by Henry Lovie.

INTERIOR OF THE TURRET OF THE UNITED STATES IRONCLAD MONITOR, "MONTAUK." Commander John L. Worden which was employed in Charleston Harbor with similar ironclads in an attack on Fort Sumter, April 7, 1863, in which the fort was scarcely harmed, while the destruction on the ironclads was very great, and one of the number, the "Weehawken," being lost. The fleet was enabled to deliver but 139 shot, while the fort directed against the ironclads 515 effective shot. From a sketch by W. T. Crane.

BATTLE OF DRANESVILLE, VA., FRIDAY MORNING, DECEMBER 20, 1861.—This engagement was planned by General McCall, commanding a division of the Army of the Potomac, in order to prevent the Confederate forces making inroads into Maryland. The troops engaged were the First Pennsylvania (Kam Rifles) known as the "Bucktails," the Sixth, Ninth, Tenth and Twelfth Regiments Pennsylvania Reserve Corps, the First Pennsylvania Artillery (Eastern Battery), and the First Pennsylvania Cavalry, Colonel Bayard. The brigade was commanded by General Ord. The Confederate forces engaged were commanded by Gen J. E. B. Stuart. The battle lasted one hour. The Federals lost 7 killed, 63 wounded and 3 prisoners. The Confederates, 90 killed, 10 wounded and 8 prisoners. This was the first important success achieved by the Army of the Potomac, and was the occasion of a special congratulating letter from Secretary Cameron.—From a sketch by Henry Lovie.

17

INVASION OF THE NORTHERN STATES. GENERAL LEE'S ARMY CROSSING THE POTOMAC, JUNE 11, 1863.—The defeat of Burnside at Fredericksburg and of Hooker at Chancellorsville had placed Lee in control of the Virginia Valley with an open road into Pennsylvania. Hooker was at Centreville protecting Washington, and Lee sought to draw him into an engagement that would divert the Federal Army from the defence of the National Capitol to resist the invasion of the Northern States. This purpose was not successful, and the slow progress of Lee's army down the valley was not seriously opposed and the Confederate Cavalry crossed the Potomac on June 11th, followed by the main army of 100,000 men in orderly and well chosen marches that occupied ten to twelve days. This movement led to the resignation of General Hooker, the appointment of General Meade and the battle of Gettysburg.—From a sketch by George Law.

18

BATTLE OF GETTYSBURG, PA., THURSDAY EVENING, JULY 2, 1863.—General Lee had succeeded in crossing the Potomac, and with an army 100,000 strong was living upon the country invaded. President Lincoln called upon the nearest States for 100,000 militia for six months' service. Before any of the militia could be brought up the battle of Gettysburg had been fought, and the danger was over. General Lee was to the North of Meade's Army, and cut off from supplies or reinforcements from Virginia, with a hostile country in front. He saw that to move farther to the North would be fatal with the Federal Army on his flank and rear. He, therefore, ordered the whole army to concentrate and move against the oncoming Federal forces. Our sketch represents the second day's fight, in which Sickles' corps played so conspicuous a part, holding Meade's extreme left. This corps lost 6,000 of the 10,000 that was the Federal loss of the second day. The Confederate loss was about the same, and the advantage at night appeared to be with neither army.—From a sketch by Edwin Forbes.

19

BATTLE AT DAM NO. 4, POTOMAC RIVER.—In the progress of General Lee's army across the Potomac in June. 1863. but little active opposition was offered. except by separate brigades or isolated cavalry skirmishers. The artist has made a picture of a stand taken near Dam No. 4 by Gen. Daniel Butterfield's brigade, where they held in check for some hours the advance of the Confederate Army and greatly harassed them. The Confederates collected their forces, however, and the Federal Army from the heights, they retreating in good order, taking their guns with them and suffering but little loss. Their shells did considerable damage in the ranks of the Confederates.—From a sketch by F. B. Schell.

20

BATTLE OF PETERSBURG, VA. JUNE 16, 1864.—Eighteenth Corps carrying a portion of Beauregard's line. General Beauregard had hastened down from Richmond and withdrawn 8,000 men from Bermuda Hundred to Petersburg, on finding that the Federal forces had full possession of all the defensive works. The Eighteenth Corps, General Smith, furiously assaulted his line on the afternoon of the 16th, the Confederates finally giving way. During a temporary absence General Beauregard learned of the breaking of his line, and he hastened to reinstate it. Just then Gracie's brigade, the last of the reinforcements from Bermuda Hundred, came up to his aid and regained their abandoned line just as night came on. They, however, withdrew under the fire of the Eighteenth Corps to a shorter inner line, and this they hastily intrenched and formed in one night's work the beginning of those great works which held in check the Federal Army before Petersburg until its final occupation, April, 1865.—From a sketch by E. F. Mullen.

BATTLEFIELD OF SECOND BULL RUN, MANASSAS JUNCTION, VA., as it appeared in August, 1863, one year after the battle.—The series of battles fought August 28th, 29th and 30th, 1862, between the Army of Northern Virginia, commanded by Gen. Robert E. Lee, and the Army of the Potomac, commanded by Gen. John Pope, was on the old battleground of First Bull Run, July 21, 1861. The fight of the 28th and 29th, known as the Battle of Groveton, and of the 30th, known as the Second Battle of Bull Run, resulted in a total rout of the Federal forces, who retreated behind Centreville to protect the Federal Capitol. The loss to the Federal troops was upwards of 14,800 and of the Confederates fully 10,700.—From a sketch by Edwin Forbes.

ADVANCE OF McCLELLAN'S ARMY FROM BIG BETHEL TO YORKTOWN, APRIL 6, 1862.—The failure of the Federal Army to gain an approach to Richmond by way of Manassas Junction determined General McClellan to transfer the Army of the Potomac to the Peninsula, landing the advance at Newport News, and taking the road of the country by way of Big Bethel and Norwich, C. H., to the rear, to co-operate with Flag Officer Goldsborough's fleet on the York River in the capture of Yorktown, and making that place the base of operations for the attack on Richmond.—From a sketch by E. S. Hall.

BATTLE OF ANTIETAM. SCENE DURING THE BOMBARDMENT, SEPTEMBER 17, 1862.—After the second Battle of Bull Run the army of General Lee remained in the neighborhood of the battlefield until September 5th and 6th, when they crossed the Potomac at Leesburg and occupied Frederick and the surrounding country. General McClellan had taken command of the defeated army of General Pope, and hastened to meet Lee on Maryland soil, following him towards the North. On the morning of the 17th the real battle was begun and lasted all day. The following morning the Confederates asked for an armistice to bury their dead, and under cover of these operations General Lee withdrew his army to the right back of the Potomac. McClellan had an army of 87,164, and Lee's forces were between 50,000 and 70,000 strong. The Federal loss was 2,100 killed, 9,416 wounded and 1,043 missing. The loss of the Confederate Army is placed at 3,000 killed and 12,000 wounded and prisoners. As the battle was fought near the village of Sharpsburg, the inhabitants were in great personal danger, as shown in the sketch by F. H. Schell.

BATTLE OF WILSON'S CREEK, MO. CHARGE OF THE FIRST IOWA REGIMENT, AUGUST 10, 1861.—Gen. Nathaniel Lyon, with an army of 5,200 men, forced the battle against a Confederate force four times larger than his own, under General McCullough. This engagement was one of the most desperate of the entire Civil War, and General Lyon was three times wounded when he was assisted to another horse, and, riding at the head of the First Iowa Regiment, he led the to the charge and received a fatal shot from a Minnie ball through the heart. The Federal loss was 223 killed, 721 wounded and 291 missing. The Confederates lost 421 killed, 1,300 wounded and gained the victory.—From a sketch by F. B. Wilkie.

ADVANCE OF GENERAL BANKS' DIVISION INTO WESTERN MARYLAND, OCTOBER, 1861.—While the two main armies of Virginia were each watching the movements of the other through their advanced pickets at Fairfax Court House General Banks, who had superseded General Patterson after the Battle of Bull Run, had been pushing his outposts from Harper's Ferry up the valley into Western Maryland. This movement was made necessary in order to protect the country from the raids made by the Confederate Army to procure supplies, they having already consumed everything in the vicinity of Centreville and Manassas. This movement resulted in the disastrous Battle of Balls Bluff. Our sketch is made as General Thomas' brigade is passing in review before General Banks and his staff.

BATTLE OF CHANCELLORSVILLE, SATURDAY, MAY 2, 1863.—Gen. Joseph Hooker had been placed in command of the Army of the Potomac in January, 1863. He had rested and recruited the troops, and in April had an effective army of 132,000 men. The Confederate forces, inspired by their recent successes, were encamped on the opposite bank of the Rappahannock, their line extending from Port Royal to a point about two miles above Fredericksburg, with two lines of retreat, one to Richmond and one to Gordonsville. General Lee had about 60,000 effective men. On the evening of the 30th of April General Hooker had advanced his entire army across the river, and established his headquarters at Chancellorsville. On the 2d of April Gen. "Stonewall" Jackson had gained the advantage, routed Howard's Corps, and was coming down upon the right flank of the main line, when General Pleasanton ordered a cavalry charge into the woods, threw into position all the artillery within reach, loaded the guns with grape and canister, depressed them so as to make the shot strike half way between the Federal line and the woods, from which the Confederates were ready to emerge, and they met the storm of iron and were effectually checked. It was at this time that General Jackson fell, and before the Confederates could maneuver for a new position night put an end to the conflict.—From a sketch by Edwin Forbes.

THE UNITED STATES NAVAL BRIGADE CONSTRUCTING THE MARINE BATTERY ON SHUTTER'S HILL, VA.—The disorganization of the Federal Army after its defeat at Bull Run in July, 1861, made it necessary to surround Washington with defensive works of great strength. When General Mansfield occupied Alexandria he had taken possession of the heights back of the town, and constructed forts to protect the Long Bridge and Acqueduct Bridge. The Naval Brigade co-operated with the army and planted the Marine battery on Shutter's Hill, so as to guard Alexandria and at the same time command the Fairfax road. This formed but one of a chain of fortifications extending on the Virginia heights opposite Washington, from Fort Corcoran to Fort Albany.—From a sketch by J. E. Hillen.

BATTLE OF THE WILDERNESS, MAY 10, 1864.—On the morning of the 10th, Hancock, who held the right of Grant's line, and who was waiting for the enemy to attack and had during the previous day fortified his position, was ordered to withdraw two divisions from the south side of the Potomac River to assist in an assault upon the enemy on Warren's front. Gibbon's and Birney's divisions were withdrawn, leaving Barlow's division on the other side of the river. As the Fifth Corps, even with the help of Hancock's two divisions, could not make an impression against Lee's line, Barlow came to their aid, but the day resulted in disaster, and both corps were repulsed with heavy sacrifice. The Sixth Corps was, however, more successful, and captured 900 prisoners and several guns; but being unsupported, General Upton, whose brigade led the assault, left the captured guns and retired in good order.—From a sketch by Edwin Forbes.

29

SURRENDER OF GENERAL JOHNSTON'S ARMY.—Scenes of the negotiations between Generals Sherman and Johnston, April 18, 1865.—General Kilpatrick, with Gen. Wade Hampton and staff, discussing the campaign.—James E. Taylor, the artist who accompanied, as a soldier. General Sherman's army in its march through Georgia to the sea, and thence through the Carolinas until they met and received the capitulation of Gen. Joseph E. Johnston and his army near Charlotte, N. C., was prevented by strict orders from General Sherman from making a sketch of the interior of the house of James Bennett, where the meeting took place, and had to content himself with the sketch, as here presented, taken while the two commanders were in conference. No sketch of that scene was ever made at the time.—From a sketch by James E. Taylor.

30

SHELLING PETERSBURG, VA.—The Ninth Army Corps played a conspicuous part in the siege and final capture of Petersburg, Va., and our artist has presented a beautiful picture of an incident of that siege, taken from the heights occupied by the Thirty-fourth New York and the Seventh Maine Batteries of Light Artillery belonging to Wilcox's third division, when engaged in shelling the City of Petersburg over the heads of the army engaged in skirmishing with the invested army.—From a sketch by A. McCallum.

A CHARACTERISTIC ARMY SCENE.—Mr. Edwin Forbes did not confine his war sketches to battle scenes, but in the picture before us gives an every-day scene in army life in an outdoor blacksmith shop.

BATTLE OF CHAMPION HILLS, MISS., MAY 16, 1863. Also known as the Battle of Baker's Creek and Edward's Station.—This engagement was between a portion of the Army of the Tennessee, commanded by Maj.-Gen. U. S Grant, and the Army of Mississippi and East Tennessee, commanded by Lieut.-Gen. John C. Pemberton. The scene of the sketch represents the defeat of the Confederate forces opposed to an advance made by the First Brigade, 12th Division, 13th Army Corps, made up of the 11th, 24th, 34th and 46th Indiana and the 29th Wisconsin regiments, commanded by General McGinnis. The battle lasted for 6¼ hours, and was mainly fought on the side of the Federal forces by Hovey's division of McClernand's corps and Logan's division of McPherson's corps. The Confederates had a force of 25,000 troops, and lost in killed and wounded about 3,000, with 2,000 prisoners and 20 guns. The Federal troops lost killed, 1,843 wounded and 189 missing. The Confederates were forced to retire to the Big Black River. From a sketch by F. B. Schell.

33

DEFENDING KENTUCKY FROM THE INVASION OF GEN. E. KIRBY SMITH.—Volunteers crossing from Cincinnati, O., to Covington, Ky., on a bridge hastily constructed of coal boats to reinforce the Federal Army occupying the State. In 1862 Gen. Edmund Kirby Smith was placed in command of the department of East Tennessee, Kentucky, North Georgia and Western North Carolina. When Gen. Braxton Bragg determined to invade Kentucky and menace the Northern States bordering on the Ohio River, General Smith led the advance, and his threat of invasion found the Federal Army in Kentucky unequal to the task of repelling his army, and volunteers were hastily called for. The sketch of our artist shows the character and determination of these volunteers. From a sketch by Henry Lovie.

BATTLE OF CEDAR MOUNTAIN, VA., AUGUST 9, 1862.—The First and Third Brigades of the First Division, Second Army Corps, driving the forces of "Stonewall" Jackson from the woods. Gen. John Pope had assumed command of the Army of Virginia, with "headquarters in the saddle," and at once directed the corps and division commanders to prepare to drive the forces of the enemy at every point. Generals Gordon and Crawford, with the First and Third Brigades of Williams' division, Banks' corps, had charged into the woods (the favorite cover of "Stonewall" Jackson in accepting battle), and our artist has caught with his pencil the successful charge. The general result of the battle was disastrous to the Federal forces, as they were greatly outnumbered, and lost nearly 2,000 in killed, wounded and prisoners, together with a large quantity of munitions of war. The Confederate forces lost about 1,300 in killed and wounded. The battle lasted two hours. From a sketch by Edwin Forbes.

35

GENERAL GRANT'S HEADQUARTERS ON THE MISSISSIPPI·RIVER ABOVE VICKSBURG.—Our artist has in this sketch preserved an incident of the campaign of General Grant, who immediately after the battle of Corinth had set about the capture of Vicksburg. On March 29, 1863, with 50,000 men, he arrived at Young's Point, opposite the mouth of the Yazoo, above Vicksburg. His "second plan" to cut a canal across the peninsula, opposite the city, had been formed at Washington and put into operation. The high water broke the levees, drowned out the camps and flooded the country, and after two months of laborious effort General Grant reported the plan impracticable, and then, after being unsuccessful in turning the current of the river (his third plan), he determined on the finally successful one of running the batteries, and thus placing the army below the city. From a sketch by Henry Lovie.

36

BATTLE OF MUMFORDSVILLE, KY., SEPTEMBER 14, 1862.—The Confederate Army, under General Bragg, had entered the State of Kentucky, August 21, 1862, determined to occupy the line of the Ohio. On the 13th of September his advance column demanded the surrender of Mumfordsville. The Federal force stationed there for the protection of the bridge was under the command of Colonel Wilder, and consisted of about 3,000 men and four guns. They were fortified and had constructed an abatis to protect the fort against assault. General Duncan, the commander of the advance of Braggs' army, made battle, and on the 14th (Sunday) succeeded in charging through the abatis. It is at this moment that Mr. Lovie made his historic sketch and saved to history a picture of actual war. After a siege of three days, in which time the Federal forces were somewhat reinforced, and after actual battle of seven hours, the Federal forces surrendered 3,566 men and 10 guns, having lost 28 men killed and 20 wounded. The Confederate loss was about 714 in killed and wounded. From a sketch by Henry Lovie.

THE SIEGE OF ATLANTA, GA. Confederate attack on General Logan's corps, July 28, 1864.—The Army of the Tennessee, now commanded by General Logan, began a movement on July 27th to strike the main road and cut off Atlanta from the South. General Hood sent Stewart to reinforce Lee's corps and intercept the movement, and the battle raged at Ezra Church the entire afternoon. The Confederates failed to dislodge the Federals from their position and retired. The Federal loss was about 572 killed and wounded. From a sketch by C. E. F. Hillen.

CONFEDERATE ARMY EVACUATING SAVANNAH, GA., upon the arrival of General Sherman, December 21, 1864.—The great "March to the Sea" had been accomplished by Sherman's army, and the almost uninterrupted progress of the victorious soldiers was not broken on their drawing near the city of Savannah by the opposition of the Confederate army of occupation, as they quietly and orderly withdrew, crossing the river on a pontoon bridge and making their way through Carolina to join the army in Virginia, but closely followed by Sherman. From a sketch by W. T. Crane.

SKIRMISH AT SALEM, MO., DECEMBER 6, 1861.—This place had been for some time occupied by a detachment of Federal troops under Major Bowen, who held it as the key to one of the probable routes of the Confederate forces in their march towards St. Louis. A considerable Confederate force, under Colonel Freeman, who was in advance of Gen. Jeff Thompson's army, made a vigorous effort to capture the place, but was repulsed with considerable loss. This prevented the reinforcement of General Price's army, which was operating in Southern Missouri and had been defeated in western portion of the State. General Pope held the north securely by his small but active force, and the Confederate forces, unable to concentrate their armies, were powerless to advance. From a sketch by Henry Lovie.

39

GENERAL BANKS' DIVISION RECROSSING THE POTOMAC from Williamsport, Md., to attack "Stonewall" Jackson, May 26, 1862.—The Federal forces in Northern Virginia were widely scattered, and invited attack from "Stonewall" Jackson as a counter-movement to McClellan's projected Peninsular campaign against Richmond. General Banks had 6,000 men at Strasburg. Fremont was 70 miles to the southwest at Franklin, and McDowell was near Fredericksburg, ready to march towards Richmond and co-operate with McClellan. Jackson had concentrated his command at Harrisburg nearer to either of these bodies than they were to each other. Banks, the nearest and weakest, interposed only by Colonel Kenly with 1,400 men at Front Royal, was made the object of Jackson's attack, who on the 23d quickly swept away Kenly's force and pushed towards Winchester, in order to gain the rear of Banks and prevent his retreat down the valley. A race between the two armies then took place for the possession of Winchester. Banks reached the place only to be driven out by Jackson, and he retreated towards Martinsburg and then pushed for the Potomac, which he crossed on the 25th at Williamsport and established himself on the Maryland shore. After gathering together his defeated army he determined to recross and attack Jackson, who had, however, prepared himself to retire rather than endanger his army, now likely to be cut off by Fremont and McDowell. From a sketch by Edwin Forbes.

BATTLE OF BENTONVILLE, N. C., MARCH 20, 1865.—This was the last orderly battle of the Civil War, and was shortly followed by the surrender of the army of General Johnston to General Sherman. Johnston had concentrated his forces of 40,000 men at Smithfield, N. C., after the battle of Averysboro' (March 16, 1865), and the army of General Sherman was on its way to Goldsboro, not expecting any further resistance. Johnston slipped out of Smithfield at night and suddenly fell upon the left wing, commanded by General Slocum, who was at first driven back, but hastily throwing up rifle-pits assumed the defensive, supported by Kilpatrick's cavalry. Six attacks were made by Johnston, who failed to dislodge the veterans of Slocum. The next morning the right wing under General Howard had arrived and found Johnston strongly entrenched. An attempt to cut off Johnston's retreat was unsuccessful, and Johnston's army escaped towards Raleigh, via Smithfield. The Federal loss was 1,600 killed and wounded. The Confederates left 267 dead on the field and 1,600 prisoners. The artist sketched the battle just as General Mower's division of the 17th Corps turned the Confederates' left. From a sketch by Joseph Becker.

MORNING DETAIL.—The Fourth New Hampshire Volunteers going to their work in the fortifications at Hilton Head, S. C. Charleston, S. C., and Savannah, Ga., were at the commencement of the Civil War strong Confederate ports, and their blockade was of prime concern to the Federal Government. After General Butler's successful occupation of the North Carolina coast the Government decided on Hilton Head and Port Royal Harbor as the most desirable points on the South Carolina coast to establish a foothold. To this end an expedition under the joint command of General Sherman and Commodore Dupont sailed from Fortress Monroe on October 29, 1861, and after slight resistance from the two forts and a land force under General Drayton took possession of Port Royal Harbor and established an important center of naval operations. The sketch made by the artist is one of the incidents of life at Hilton Head shortly after its occupation. From a sketch by W. T. Crane.

HOWLETT'S CONFEDERATE BATTERY SHELLING THE FEDERAL IRONCLADS ON THE JAMES RIVER, VA.—The James River above Bermuda Hundred makes a double bend, first to the west, then south, thence east, and after a curve of six miles returns to within less than half a mile of its starting point. This tortuous bend was commanded by Confederate batteries, which barred the farther ascent of the river. General Butler, in command of the Army of the James, engaged in digging a canal through the narrow isthmus, by which gunboats could ascend the river and possibly force a passage to Richmond. The work was done largely by colored troops protected by the Federal gunboats. The artist makes his sketch from the position of the Confederate battery. From a sketch by A. McCallum.

GENERAL FREMONT'S ARMY ON ITS MARCH FROM TIPTON TO WARSAW, OCTOBER 15TH, 1861.

GENERAL FREMONT'S ARMY FORDING THE OSAGE RIVER AT WARSAW, MO., OCTOBER 18, 1861.—The defeat of the Federal forces under Colonel Mulligan at Lexington alarmed Fremont, and he hastened to Jefferson City to prepare to attack Price, who had retired to Springfield to bring himself in easy communication with Arkansas and at the same time tempt Fremont from his source of supplies. In the march of Fremont's army they took a route on the north of the Osage River to Tipton, and thence to Warsaw, the first available ford, and crossing the river here, they made Springfield on October 27, 1861. Our artist has sketched the army on its march from Tipton to Warsaw, and again as the troops are fording the river. From a sketch by Henry Lovie.

THE NINTH ARMY CORPS charging into the crater at Petersburg, Va., July 30, 1864.—Assault of General James H. Ledlie's brigade after the explosion of the mine. The assaulting party was chosen by lot from the colored troops of the Ninth corps and fell upon Ledlie. His men dashed over the lip of the crater immediately upon the lifting of the smoke from the explosion and plunged wildly into its depths, then found to be a yawning chasm 135 feet long, 97 feet wide, and 30 feet deep. The explosion had buried the Confederate batteries and separated the troops on either side of the crater, where they reorganized, as brigade after brigade followed into the crater, crowded in disorganized mass. A hand-to-hand fight ensued, when a cross fire from the Confederate batteries effectually emptied the crater; only 30 men and three stands of color were captured. General Meade reported 4,400 killed, wounded, and missing. General Beauregard gives the Confederate loss as 1,172. From a sketch by A. McCallum.

A RAILROAD BATTERY ON THE BALTIMORE AND OHIO RAILROAD, built to protect the workmen while rebuilding the burned bridges fired by the Southern sympathizers to prevent the passage of troops to the defense of Washington. The opposition to the invasion of the Slave States by the Federal Army was so decided at the outbreak of the Civil War that the bridges were all destroyed between Washington and Baltimore, and even above that city. The first troops reached Washington by way of Annapolis and a forced march across the country. After the occupation of Baltimore, Md., by General Butler, the railroads were hastily rejoined, and the artist shows one of the devices to protect the workmen. From a sketch by A. Berghaus.

CHARGE OF FREMONT'S BODY GUARD UNDER MAJOR ZAGONYI NEAR SPRINGFIELD. MO., OCTOBER 25, 1861.—In the march of Fremont's army into Southwestern Missouri he had divided it into five divisions, commanded by Generals Hunter. Pope, Sigel. Asboth and McKinstry, who were directed to press closely upon Price's retreat. Sigel was sent forward and met the Confederates near Springfield. where he made his two ever-memorable charges, leading his men in the face of a murderous fire and driving the enemy through the town. Just at this crisis Fremont was succeeded by Hunter, Springfield was abandoned, and Price recovered the ground gained by Fremont. From a sketch by Henry Lovie.

PASSAGE DOWN THE OHIO RIVER OF GENERAL NEGLEY'S BRIGADE.—At the outbreak of the Civil War Gen. James S. Negley, who had served throughout the war with Mexico, raised a brigade of three months' volunteers, the 77th, 78th and 79th Pennsylvania Regiments, under Colonels Hamlight, Stambargh and Sewall. and in April, 1861, transported his brigade on six steamers down the Ohio River to join the Army of the Ohio, where he did good service in protecting the State of Kentucky from invasion.   At the battle of Lavergne, October 7, 1862, he greatly distinguished himself, his command defeating the Confederates under Anderson and Forrest.   The next month he was made a major-general for gallantry at Stone River.   From a sketch by Henry Lovie.

BLOWING OUT THE BULKHEAD OF THE DUTCH GAP CANAL, JAMES RIVER, VA.—Farrar's Island in the James River was in January, 1865, a peninsula formed by the circuitous course of the river and was the scene of the explosion, as illustrated by the artist in the above sketch. The canal, planned by General Butler and executed under Major P. S. Michie, was commenced August 15, 1864, and finished January 1, 1865. Its purpose was not only to shorten the navigation of the river some seven miles, but to avoid the Confederate batteries planted at Howlett's House in the curve of the river. The final work was the blowing out of the clay bulkheads by powder, but the substance fell back and obstructed the passage. The canal was of no practical service during the war, but has since been put to use in navigating the river. From a sketch by J. E. Taylor.

GENERAL McCLELLAN AND HIS ARMY PASSING THROUGH FREDERICK CITY, MD., in pursuit of the Confederate Army, September 12, 1862.—The Confederate Army under General Lee had crossed the Potomac, near Leesburg, on the 4th, 5th and 6th of September, 1862, and had occupied Frederick and the surrounding country along the Minococey.   General McClellan threw a part of his army between the enemy and the fords of the Potomac, and thus forced Lee to evacuate Frederick City on the 10th and march towards Hagerstown.   General McClellan, in person, followed the retreating army, and our artist has given us an evidence of the enthusiastic reception given to the Federal commander as he marched through the street of the town at the head of his troops.   From a sketch by Edwin Forbes.

GENERAL BANKS' ARMY IN THE ADVANCE ON SHREVEPORT, LA., CROSSING CANE RIVER, MARCH 31, 1864.—This incident in the Red River campaign illustrates the strategy and care exercised in a march through the enemies' country surrounded by dangers seen and unseen.   By a skillful maneuver the commanding general was able to throw his entire army across the Cane River, and thus elude the pursuit of the enemy. unsupplied with ponton bridges to follow, and protected by the gunboats of Porter's fleet, to take up the march towards Shreveport.   The subsequent disasters of the campaign and its final abandonment are matters of history.   From a sketch by C. E. H. Bonwill.

THE NAVAL PRACTICE BATTERY AT THE UNITED STATES NAVY YARD, WASHINGTON, D. C.—Of all the arms in the service employed in the Civil War, it is probable that none took a more conspicuous part than the batter especially when directed from the deck of gunboats against other boats or against forts. At Belmont the gunboats saved Grant's army from defeat. At Pittsburg Landing the presence of gunboats rendered the only help that made defeat le disastrous. In all the campaigns of the Western rivers a gunboat was worth more than a regiment of men. The practice given at the Navy Yard at Washington schooled gunners for this service, and sent out men trained to do deadly execu tion with shot and shell. From a sketch by W. E. Crane.

GENERAL VIEW OF FORTS HATTERAS AND CLARK WHEN CAPTURED, AUGUST 29, 1861, by the united military and naval forces under Gen. B. F. Butler and Commodore Strigham.—After a heavy bombardment, lasting from 9 A M. until night, Fort Clark was evacuated; the flag of Fort Hatteras was also hauled down. In the morning the assault on Fort Hatteras was resumed and soon a white flag was displayed, and Commander Barron offered to surrender conditionally. General Butler demanded unconditional surrender, which terms were finally accepted. The importance of Hatteras inlet to the Government was very great at this time. From a sketch by W. E Crane.

53

BATTLE OF CEDAR CREEK, VA., OCTOBER 19, 1864.—The Confederate Army under General Early driving back the Sixth, Eighth and Nineteenth Federal Army Corps, under General Wright, on the morning of October 19, 1864.—From point to point they were driven back before the furious rush of Kershaw in front, while Gordon and Ramsear poured in a fire on their left flank. The camps of the Eighth and Nineteenth corps were in possession of the Confederates, and what remained of the corps were pushed back on the Sixth, which alone maintained the fight. This also finally fell back and all retreated for three miles, where General Wright began at nine o'clock to form his broken lines. They were beaten, but not routed. From a sketch by J. E. Taylor.

BATTLE OF MIDDLETOWN, VA., OCTOBER 19, 1864.—After the defeat of the morning and while the fugitives were still fleeing, they met Sheridan on his historic black steed riding from Winchester to the scene of real conflict. His presence restored order, and the Sixth Corps, not yet wholly panic stricken as were the others, with Getty far in the front still confronting the enemy, momentarily expecting an attack. The other divisions of Wright and Emery were brought forward. At four o'clock the order came from Sheridan to advance. The whole Federal force rushed forward and swept the Confederates before them, and so utterly destroyed was Early's army that there was nothing left worth pursuing. From a sketch by J. E. Taylor.

BOMBARDMENT OF FORTS JACKSON AND ST. PHILLIP BY THE FEDERAL MORTAR SCHOONERS. The First Division of the squadron preparing for action, April 20, 1862.—Our artist, William Waud, occupied a position at the masthead of the United States Steamer Mississippi, and preserves to history this correct representation of the procession of vessels as they prepared to run the gauntlet of the two formidable forts built to protect the river and the city of New Orleans. On the extreme left may be seen the Confederate steamers stationed above the forts and around the bend of the river, next the smoke from the fire rafts, as they are floating down with the tide to destroy the attacking fleet. Then the outlines of Fort Jackson and below it Fort St. Phillip, with the Confederate flag floating from its flagstaff. The mortar schooners, with their masts disguised with cedar bushes, are close in shore near the fort, while others on the opposite bank are firing shell from the distance into the forts. The procession of Federal vessels nearest the shore is led by the Kineo, followed by the Harriet Lane (Porter's flagship), Westfield and Mississippi, while in the center of the river the Hartford (Farragut's flagship) leads, followed by the Cayuga and Pensacola, with the Iroquois far in the advance engaging the forts, and the Oneida between the two lines.

WHEELER'S CONFEDERATE CAVALRY ATTACKING A FEDERAL SUPPLY TRAIN, NEAR JASPER, TENN.—The Chattanooga campaign planned against Bragg's army, and which led to the battle of Chickamauga and final disaster to the Federal army, was precipitated by orders from Washington to General Rosecrans to advance and report daily to General Hallock at Washington. The movement of the main army was begun August 16, 1863. Two of Crittenden's columns crossed the Cumberland Mountains into the Sequatchie Valley, and while his supply train was following the route of the army they were attacked and captured by Wheeler's Cavalry, who were constantly hanging on the rear of the advancing army, and by dashing down out of some mountain retreat, capturing whole wagon trains. It was one of these attacks that our artist has pictured, and it tells its own story of one phase of army life. From a sketch by J. F. E. Hillen.

RETURN OF A FORAGING PARTY WITH THEIR SPOILS TO BATON ROUGE, LA., with captured horses, carts, wagons, mules, provisions, contrabands, etc. When Farragut's fleet had passed the forts and advanced up the river, the Iroquois, under Commander Palmer, arrived off Baton Rouge, May 7, 1862, and demanded the surrender of the place, which, not being defended by any Confederate force, was speedily granted. On occupying the city the Federal troops, just released from a long sea voyage, found especial enjoyment in the foraging expeditions made out in the surrounding country. Our artist has made a spirited sketch of a returning party, which will be recognized by every veteran soldier. From a sketch by J. H. Schell.

BATTLE OF FRAZIER'S FARM OR CHARLES CITY ROAD, VA., MONDAY, JUNE 30, 1862.—On Sunday, June 29th, McClellan had fought the battle of Savages' Station. His line was on the morning of the 30th stretched eight miles long, from White Oak Swamp to Malvern Hill on the James. Protected by this line his artillery and trains were slowly retreating through the mud. General Lee's purpose was to make an attack in column on this long line, break through the center, hurl the left back upon "Stonewall" Jackson, and assault the right in the rear. To accomplish this strategic movement required his whole strength, about 80,000 men. The plan failed. Only about 18,000 men made the attack, and the grand and decisive battle planned by Lee resulted in a series of undecisive combats. The reports of the several generals on both sides differ greatly in their accounts of this battle, which closed with the darkness, and the Federal forces continued their retreat towards Malvern Hill. From a sketch by William Waud.

RHODE ISLAND REGIMENTS EMBARKING AT PROVIDENCE FOR WASHINGTON, VIA NEW YORK.—Within five days after President Lincoln's call for 75,000 troops, the Rhode Island marine artillery, with 8 guns and 110 horses, passed through New York on their way to Washington, and the First Regiment of Infantry, 1,200 strong, under Col. Ambrose E. Burnside, was also ready to move. The young and patriotic Democratic Governor, William Sprague, had from his private purse armed and equipped the regiment, and the State appropriated half a million of dollars for equipping volunteers. The Governor, Lieutenant Governor and representatives of $30,000,000 of wealth made up this first volunteer regiment from Rhode Island, ready within five days to do effective service in the field. From a sketch by J. H. Schell.

BATTLE OF REAM'S STATION, VA., AUGUST 25, 1864.—Desperate efforts of the Confederate forces to regain possession of the Weldon Railroad. On the 21st of August, 1864 Hancock had destroyed the railroad as far south as Ream's Station. On the 25th Gibbon's Division was to continue the destruction as far as Rowanty Creek. He had scarcely left his entrenchments at Ream's Station when he was attacked by a Confederate force under Generals A. P. Hill and Wade Hampton. Hancock withdrew Gibbon's Division within the entrenchments, placing it on the left of the First Division, commanded by General Miles, who checked three successive attacks. The Confederates then opened an artillery fire on the breastworks, and by an impetuous rush broke through Miles' line, and the command gave way in confusion, leaving the artillery in the hands of the enemy. Hancock ordered Gibbon's Division to retake the guns and lost position, but they failed, and Hancock, failing to receive reinforcements, withdrew, with a loss of 2,400 in killed, wounded and missing, out of a total command of only 8,000. From a sketch by Joseph Becker.

BATTLE OF CARRICK'S FORD, VA., JULY 13, 1861.—General McClellan had assumed command of the Federal Army in Western Virginia, and had already gained decided advantages over the Confederate Army commanded by General Garnett. At Red Mountain Garnett had posted Colonel Pegram with 3,000 men, while he occupied Laurel Hill with about 8,000. General McClellan ordered Morris to occupy Garnett's forces by direct attack, while he divided his force into **two** columns, one under Colonel Rosecrans to attack the rear of Pegram, while he remained in front ready to attack simultaneously. A Federal messenger captured by the Confederates disclosed the plan, and Garnett left his intrenchments, proceeded South where he met Pegram's army, and finding their retreat cut off were obliged to follow the course of the Cheet River to the Northwest. On a bluff at the bend of the river the Confederates made a stand, but were dislodged, **and** when Garnett attempted to make another stand, about a quarter of a mile further up, while rallying his men, he was mortally wounded by **a** minie ball, and Pegram surrendered to McClellan. From a sketch by J. H. Schell.

OCCUPATION OF WRIGHTSVILLE, PA., BY GENERAL LEE'S ARMY and destruction of the Columbia Railroad bridge by the Federal forces, June 28, 1863.—The line of march of the armies of Lee and Meade into Pennsylvania was nearly parallel to the mountains between them, and each commander knowing little of the movements of the other. Lee was considerably northward of Meade. Ewell, in advance, was as far as Carlisle, preparing to move upon Harrisburg. Longstreet and Hill held Chambersburg. Fearing being cut off from his line of supply, Lee determined to fall back towards Gettysburg, not knowing that Meade had fixed upon the same place as a battlefield. In the movement from Chambersburg General Ewell's forces moved down the country, and on June 28, 1863, outposts of his army marched into Wrightsville, on the Susquehanna River, and the fleeing Federal guard in the place crossed the bridge, burning it after them to prevent pursuit. From a sketch by A. Berghaus.

62

OESTRUCTION OF THE PRIVATEER "NASHVILLE" BY THE FEDERAL IRONCLAD "MONTAUK," Capt. J. R. Worden, in the Ogeechee River, Georgia, February 28, 1863.—In October, 1861, the Nashville, commanded by Lieutenant Pegram, escaped from Charleston. She went to Southampton, England, in January, 1862, blockaded by the United States Steamer Tuscarora. The British Government gave the privateer twenty-four hours' time before allowing the Tuscarora to follow. March 1, 1862, the Nashville brought to the Confederacy $3,000,000 worth of stores. Just one year after her arrival and after she had run the blockade at Beaufort, she was destroyed in the Ogeechee River, Georgia, by the United States ironclads, the Montauk, commanded by Captain Worden, leading the attack. She was at anchor under the guns of Fort McAllister, and, shortly after being attacked, she ran aground and her magazine exploded. From a sketch by W. T. Crane.

CONTRABANDS COMING INTO THE FEDERAL CAMP IN VIRGINIA.—The negroes of the South constituted one-eighth of the entire population. They universally looked upon the war as the means for their emancipation, and they were not surprised when their freedom was proclaimed. They waited, but did not strike one blow in their own behalf. When they came within the Federal lines they became willing conscripts. About 175,000 negroes entered the United States service, the larger portion being employed in garrison duty. During the whole course of the Civil War not one case of servile insurrection occurred in the South. Mr. Forbes makes a characteristic sketch of these "contrabands" coming into the Federal camp in the plantation wagon, with an illy-matched team made up of horse, mule and ox. From a sketch by Edwin Forbes.

CAPTURE OF FORT DE RUSSY, LA., MARCH 15, 1864.—A portion of Porter's fleet accompanied the transports down the Atchafalaya and covered the landing of troops at Simmesport. Dick Taylor's force retreated to Fort De Russy, followed by A. I. Smith's command, and the gun boats returned to the Red River. When the fleet approached the fort General Smith assaulted the works and captured the garrison of 250 men and 8 guns. He had marched 28 miles, spent two hours building a bridge, engaged the enemy for two hours, and captured the only fortified position held by the Confederate forces below Shreveport, all in one day. Two days afterwards the fleet reached Shreveport. From a sketch by C. E. H. Bonwill.

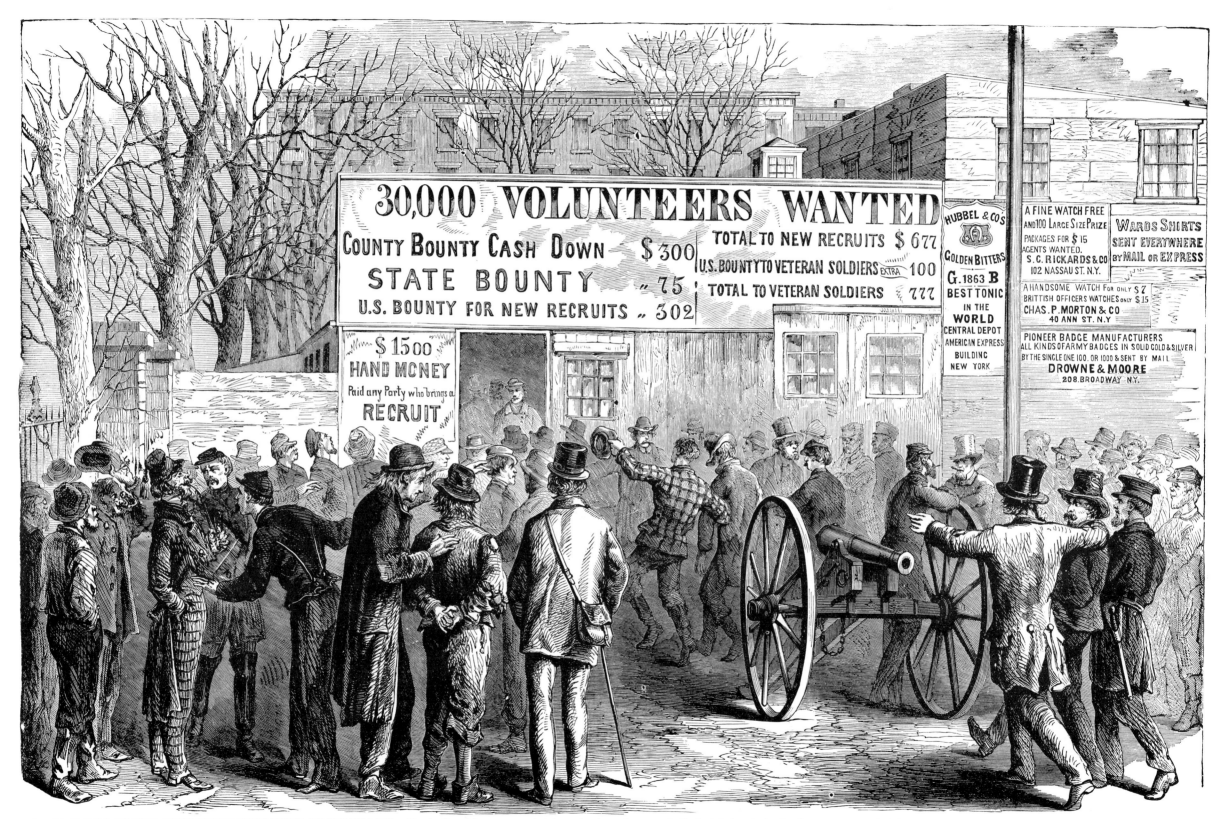

RECRUITING IN THE NEW YORK CITY HALL PARK IN 1864.—The draft and its consequent riots and universal unpopularity had induced the local governments of cities, counties and states to offer generous bounties for volunteer soldiers, and a lively business sprung up and generous rivalry arose between different localities to secure desirable recruits. The legends on the sign boards above the recruiting offices show the liberal bounties offered and the especial bonus given to veteran soldiers to induce them to re-enlist. The brokers' part in this business is shown by the side sign. From a sketch by George Law.

BATTLE OF BELMONT, MO., OPPOSITE COLUMBUS, KY., NOVEMBER 7, 1861.—Federal forces commanded by Gen. U. S. Grant; Confederates, by Gen. Leonidas Polk. From a sketch by an officer of General Grant's Army engaged in the battle.

EXPLANATION : 1. Brigadier-general Grant and Staff directing the movements of the troops.—2. Brigadier-general McClernand leading the charge at the head of the Thirty-first Illinois.—3. Thirty-first Illinois. Colonel Logan.—4. Body of Lieutenant-colonel Wendtz, Seventh Iowa.—5. Body of Captain Pulaski, Aide-de-Camp to McClernand, killed while leading the charge.—6. Caisson ordered to the field from the rear.—7. Twenty-seventh Illinois, Colonel Buford. taking the camp colors of the Confederates.—8 Thirtieth Illinois, Colonel Fouke.—8 a. Twenty-second Illinois, Colonel Dougherty.—9. Light artillery, Captain Taylor.—10. Seventh Iowa, Colonel Lamon.—11. Captain Schwartz, Acting Chief of Artillery, taking the Confederate battery.—12. Watson's Louisiana field battery.—13. Confederate artillery horses.—14. Battery of heavy ordnance at Columbus.—15. Encampment near Columbus.—16. Confederate ferryboat.—17. Columbus.

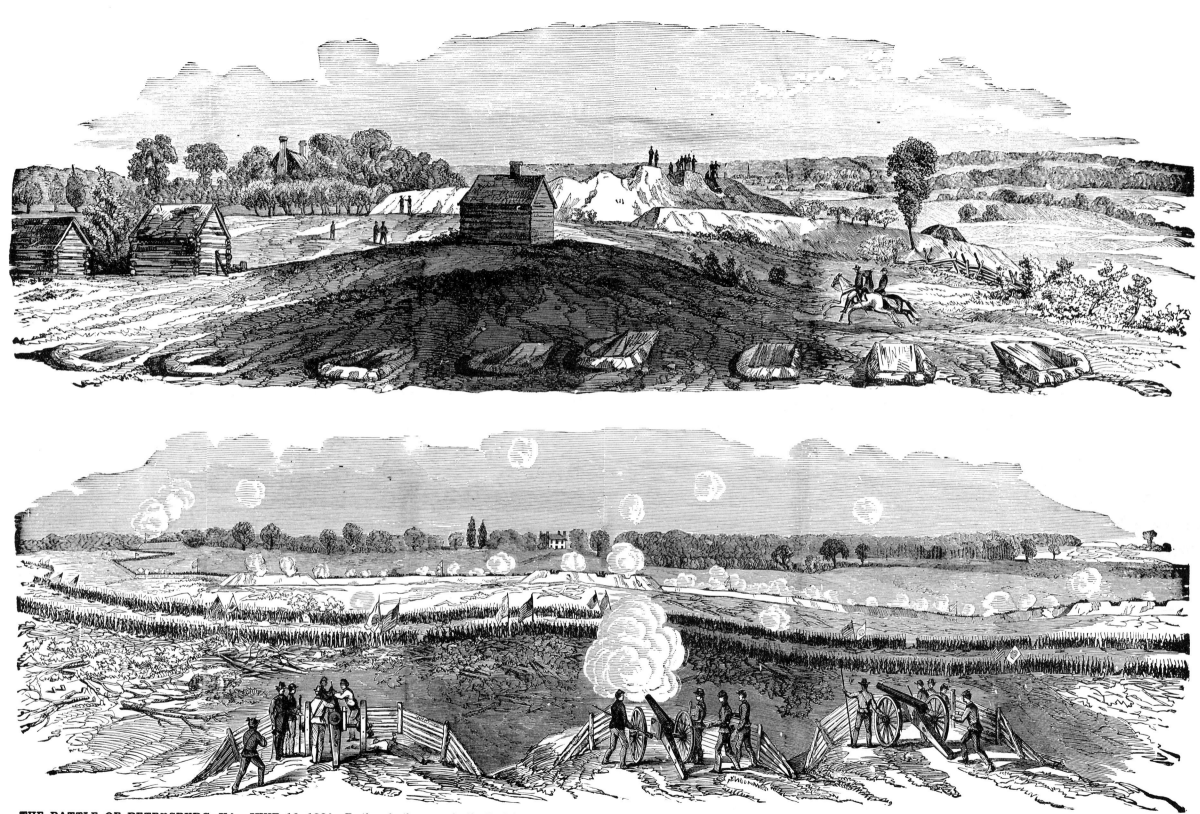

THE BATTLE OF PETERSBURG, VA., JUNE 16, 1864.—Earthworks thrown up by the Confederate left and behind which they withstood the assaults of the 18th Army Corps, commanded by General Smith, until they were overwhelmed by superior numbers and driven from their position.—The Ninth Corps, commanded by Ambrose E Burnside, charging the Confederate position on the right of their line of defense. The engagement lasted three hours, and Egan's brigade of Birney's division effected a lodgment. The contest continued in the night and then gradually slackened. From sketches by Edwin Forbes.

THE ELEVENTH PENNSYLVANIA CAVALRY COVERING THE ESCAPE OF FEDERAL PRISONERS FROM LIBBY PRISON, Richmond, Va., between October, 1863, and March, 1864.—There were at no time more than 7,000 effective troops, while fully 10,000 Federal prisoners were known to be confined in the military prisons. Several plans were formed to make a sudden dash upon the Confederate capital and release these prisoners. General Butler, on the 7th of February, 1864, sent a considerable body of cavalry from Yorktown towards Richmond. Tidings of the expedition preceded them, the roads were obstructed, and the plan failed. General Kilpatrick, with 4,000 cavalry, crossed the Rapidan, passed Spottsylvania C. H., and pushed towards Richmond. On March 1st he reached within four miles of the city, penetrated the two outer lines, rescued some fugitive prisoners fleeing from Libby prison, and concluding the enterprise not feasible, retreated to Yorktown. From a sketch by an officer.

Emmettsburg, Md. Gen. Meade's Army pursuing Gen. Lee.

BATTLE OF GETTYSBURG, PA., JULY 3, 1863.—Desperate attack of the Confederate forces after gaining the hill and passing the cemetery gate. Confederate Generals Pickett, Kemper and Armistead had scaled the walls on Cemetery Hill planted their standard upon the wall and charged through cemetery gate upon the Federal batteries. The advance of the Confederates was made with great impetuosity, and Armistead succeeded in capturing one of the Federal batteries, but Hancock, ordering forward two brigades, arrested further progress, when Stannard's forces, having rapidly changed front, advanced against Pickett's right flank and forced the Confederates to surrender. From a sketch by Edwin Forbes.

CONSTRUCTION OF FLOATING MORTAR BATTERIES BY THE FEDERAL GOVERNMENT AT THE UPPER FERRY, ST. LOUIS, MO.—The importance of a navy on our Western rivers was early appreciated. A month after the capture of Fort Sumter Commander John Rodgers was summonned to Washington, and to him was assigned the duty of creating such a navy. In the early stages of the undertaking the War Department under Secretary Cameron assumed the expense and supervision, but in the autumn of 1861 the matter was transferred to the Navy Department. Nine iron-clad gunboats and thirty-eight mortar-boats were hastily constructed at St. Louis, and in February, 1862, were brought to take part in the capture of Forts Henry and Donaldson. From a sketch by H. Lovie.

ARRIVAL OF McCLELLAN TO TAKE PERSONAL COMMAND OF THE ARMY OF THE POTOMAC IN ITS ADVANCE ON FRANKLIN, VA., APRIL 3, 1862.—The condition of the roads not being favorable to an advance of the army of the Potomac by way of Centerville and Manassas, the army was transferred to Fortress Monroe and began its march to Richmond by the way of Yorktown and West Point. General McClellan reached Fortress Monroe on the 2d of April, where he found 58,000 men and much of his artillery. The following day he moved his whole army towards Yorktown in order to prevent the reinforcement of Magruder by Johnston and expecting the co-operation of the naval force in Hampton Roads to reduce the Confederate batteries both on the James and York Rivers. The sketch of our artist shows the enthusiasm of the troops as their commander rides through the lines. From a sketch by E. S. Hale.

RECEPTION OF THE WOUNDED SOLDIERS OF THE FEDERAL ARMY AT FORTRESS MONROE, VA., during the progress of the seven days' battles before Richmond.—Cars carrying the wounded to the hospitals; surgeons dressing the wounds. The sketch of Mr. Schell tells its own story. The scene had a daily repetition during the entire week, and as fast as the boats and cars brought the disabled down the river they were cared for at the temporary hospital, and sent North by steamers to receive the best care at the hospitals at Washington, Philadelphia and New York. From a sketch by J. H. Schell.

SHERMAN'S "BUMMERS" FORAGING IN SOUTH CAROLINA ON THEIR MARCH FROM SAVANNAH TO WASHINGTON, 1865.—As the army subsisted on the enemy's country the soldiers were often guilty of much thoughtless but culpable wrong in the destruction of property that they could not use and that could in no way afford aid and comfort to the enemy. History has established that this wanton destruction was not countenanced by the commanders but the act of army followers and irregular soldiers, elated by their success and the prospects of the speedy overthrow of the secession movement. From a sketch by J. E. Taylor.

THE ENGAGEMENT AT BEALINGTON, VA., JULY 8, 1861.—General McClellan, in command of the Federal forces at North West Virginia, had about 20,000 available men and had divided them into three detachments. One of these under Gen. T. A. Morris, was sent towards Beverly and encamped at Bealington, a village at the foot of Laurel Hill and in close proximity to Garrett's position, whom he had been ordered to engage in a series of feints to distract him from the main Federal attacks directed to the rear of Garrett's forces, which consisted of about 11,000 men, including 3,000 under Colonel Pegran, at Rich Mountain. Skirmishes were kept up, those of the 8th of July being a considerable battle. The troops engaged on the Federal side were the Ninth Indiana and Fourteenth Ohio regiments. The fierceness of the attacks of the Indiana soldiers caused the Confederates to dub them "Swamp Devils," and also "The Tigers of the Bloody Ninth." This engagement was followed by the battles of Carrick Ford and Rich Mountain.—From a sketch by H. Lovie.

MANASSAS JUNCTION, VA., after its evacuation by the Confederate army, subsequent to the first battle of Bull Run, July, 1861.—Abandoned fortifications, camps, wagons and burned railroad depots. Mr. Forbes has in this sketch given a picture of desolation and ruin incident to an abandoned battle field. Here had been encamped for months the great army of Northern Virginia, and here had been won to the Southern arms their first great victory. When McClellan moved his army from their front and took up his march to Richmond by way of the York and James Rivers, the Confederates hastily broke camp and marched to the defense of their Capitol, leaving the desolate field to be occupied by the outposts of the Federal forces, left to make a feint of resistance in their front. From a sketch by Edwin Forbes.

THE FEDERAL ARMY ENTERING RICHMOND, VA., APRIL 3, 1865.—Reception of the Union troops on Main street amid the ruins of the burned city fired by the orders of General Ewell.—General Weitzel sent forward a squad of cavalry, about forty strong, whose coming aroused the cry of "The Yankees," which was taken up and repeated throughout the whole city. The crowd fled up the main street and into the by-streets, leaving only the negroes to greet the incoming soldiers. The stars and stripes were hoisted on the flagstaff of the Capitol by Lieut. Johnston de Peyster—the same flag that had floated over the headquarters of General Butler at New Orleans. The cavalry was followed by all troops marching in order with cheers and martial music. From a sketch by Joseph Becker.

VIEW FROM LONDON HEIGHTS, VA., showing Harper's Ferry, Maryland Heights, Bolivar, etc.—The Potomac coming from the North meets the Shenandoah ranging from the West at the foot of a spur of the Blue Ridge known as Elk Mountain. The united streams have torn a narrow passage through the montain, apparently separating it from summit to base, leaving almost perpendicular sides one thousand feet high. The eastern cliff is Maryland Heights, the western, or the Virginia side, London Heights. In the angle of the junction of the rivers is an elevated plateau falling steeply towards the Potomac and sloping gently towards the Shenandoah. The ridge of this plateau is Bolivar Heights, and at its foot is the village of Harper's Ferry where the first tragedy of the war for the abolition of African slavery was enacted when John Brown was hung. From a sketch by Frank H. Schell.

3

CUMBERLAND HEIGHTS, TENNESSEE, FROM THE KENTUCKY SIDE.—The narrow pass through the Cumberland Mountains known as the Gap is on the exact line between Kentucky and Tennessee at the western extremity of Virginia. As a strong strategic point it was strongly fortified by the Confederates at the commencement of the Civil War. It was abandoned by them January 18, 1862, and occupied by the Federal forces under Gen. G. W. Morgan. In August, 1862, Gen. E. Kirby Smith outflanked their position by a march through Big Creek Gap, and compelled General Morgan to abandon and destroy the works. On September 9, 1863, General Frazer, who held the Gap by a brigade of Buckner's troops, surrendered after a siege of four days to General Burnside. The Gap itself is a cliff 500 feet deep, and in some places only wide enough for a wagon road. From a sketch by an engineer of Bragg's army.

79

Chambersburg Pa

THE CONFEDERATE CAVALRY CHARGING THROUGH THE STREETS OF CHAMBERSBURG, PA.—On the 30th of July, 1863, a body of Confederate Cavalry, under command of General McCausland, entered the town of Chambersburg, Pa., and laid it under tribute of $200,000 in gold or $500,000 in currency, which demand not being complied with, he burned the town. About two-thirds of the place was destroyed, 2,500 persons were deprived of homes, and property to the value of $1,000,000 destroyed. From a sketch by Geo. Law.

80

BATTLE OF WILLIAMSBURG, VA., FOUGHT MAY 7, 1862.—Early in May Williamsburg was occupied by the Federals, while Johnston's army was beyond the Chickahominy. When the main army came up General Stoneman was sent with Smith's division to open the road to Franklin. The Confederates belonging to the rear guard of Johnston's retreating forces attempted to drive off the Federals, but were met by the Sixteenth, Thirty-first and Thirty-second and the Ninety-fifth and Ninety-sixth Pennsylvania Regiments, which kept up for nearly four hours a sharp musketry fire through the woods until they received the cannon landed by the gunboats. With the aid of the batteries then landed the Federals soon drove away the Confederates, and thereafter held the position as an additional base of supplies for the army of the Potomac. The sketch is by a soldier on the field.

RETURN OF WOUNDED SOLDIERS.—Fifty-seven wounded soldiers of the National Army captured at Bull Run were returned under a flag of truce. The scene represents their arrival on board the United States steamer "Louisiana," and the welcome given them by their companions in arms.

98

FIRST CHARGE OF FREMONT'S BODY GUARD AT SPRINGFIELD, MO., OCTOBER 25, 1861.—Toward the end of September, Fremont set out to prevent the contemplated junction of Price with the forces raised by McCullough in Arkansas. When he arrived at Warsaw he was joined by a squadron of cavalry called "Prairie Scouts" under the leadership of F. S. White. Learning that a Confederate force had just been established at Springfield, Fremont ordered Maj. Charles Zagonyi, commanding his body guard of cavalry, to take it with Major White's Scouts on a reconnoissance, and to capture the camp if deemed practicable. Major White being too ill to march as rapidly as the rest, Major Zagonyi reached the camp with only 150 men, but rather than await their arrival Zagonyi determined to meet the disparity in force and to make an immediate attack. They dashed into the force against them and drove them in wild disorder; 50 men of White's force then came up, and a second charge was made through the streets of Springfield. Zagonyi's loss was eighty four dead and wounded in this engagement, which for boldness and rapidity certainly has few parallels in any history. Sketched by Henry Lovie.

RETURN OF THE SIXTY-NINTH REGIMENT.—This regiment, composed entirely of Irish citizens, upon its return to New York city after a three months' service in the field was escorted through the streets by the Seventh Regiment and afterwards given a reception that any organization might envy.

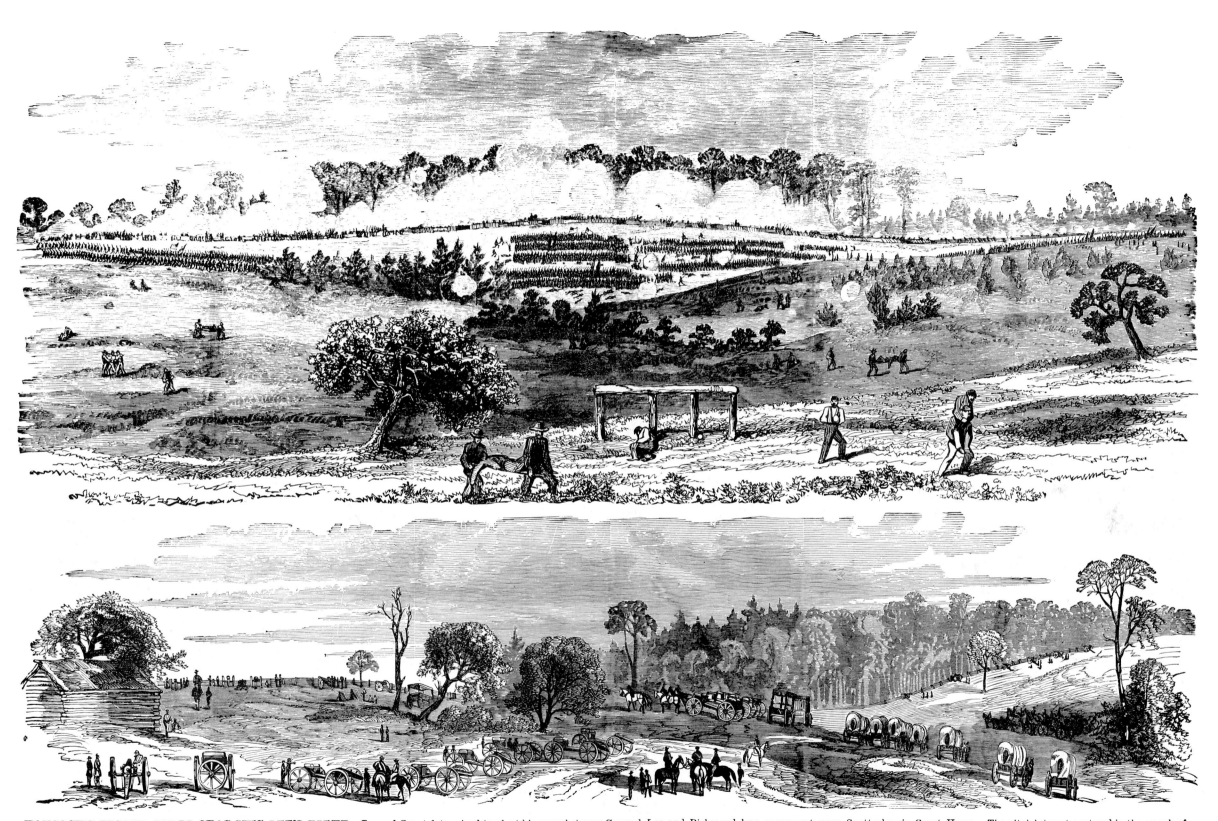

HANCOCK'S SECOND CORPS CHARGING LEE'S RIGHT.—General Grant determined to plant his army between General Lee and Richmond by a movement upon Spottsylvania Court House. The vital interest centered in the march of Warren to seize this place. After considerable fighting the column under Warren emerged from the woods into a clearing and waited for Sedgwick to come up before making an attack. In consequence of this delay Lee had managed to place himself across Grant's path and, having drawn upon the Spottsylvania Ridge a bulwark of defense, he was able to hold the Army of the Potomac in check. The next morning Hancock was ordered to attack a hill held by the Confederates in front of Warren's line. The attack upon this position had already been essayed by both the Second and the Fifth Corps, with disastrous results. When Hancock's division joined the Fifth an assault was made, May 12, 1864. The column formed on clear ground, advanced without firing a shot. When half-way toward the enemy the men broke into a ringing cheer, and on the double quick rolled like a resistless wave into the Confederate works and carried the line at all points. Sketch by Edwin Forbes.

85

BAGGAGE TRAIN.—A striking incident. The drivers of the baggage train attached to General Pleasanton's Cavalry Brigade watering their mules in the Rappahannock River.

86

THE BATTLE OF CROSS KEYS, SHENANDOAH VALLEY, SUNDAY, JUNE 8, 1862.—Opening of the fight. The Federal troops, under General Fremont, advancing to attack the Confederate army, commanded by General Jackson, posted in the wood, with its front extending for two miles. Gen. R. H. Milroy leading the center, Gen. Robert C. Schenck the right, and Generals Louis Blenker and Julius H. Stahl the left wing of the advancing army, consisting of the Eighth New York Volunteers (First German Rifles), Colonel Wutschell; Twenty-ninth New York Volunteers (German), Colonel Sorst; Forty-first New York Volunteers (De Kalb), Colonel Giza; Forty-fifth New York Volunteers Fifth German Rifles), Colonel Von Amsberg; Twenty-fifth Ohio Volunteers, Colonel Jones; Eighty-second Ohio Volunteers, Colonel Canterell; Eighth Virginia, Sixtieth Ohio and Thirty-ninth New York Volunteers, under Colonels Cluseret and D'Utassy. From a sketch by Edwin Forbes.

BURNING OF THE UNITED STATES ARSENAL AT HARPER'S FERRY, APRIL 18, 1861, by the United States troops to prevent its falling into the hands of the insurgent troops, who endeavored to seize it. Lieut. R. Jones had only a small detachment and upon the approach of the enemy set fire to trains of gunpowder previously laid. Lieutenant Jones then crossed the Potomac and fled up the canal, crossed the hills and escaped. His act was highly commended by the Government.

CAPTURE OF THE PROPELLER "FANNY."—An important entrance to Pamlico Sound was open south of Fort Hatteras, defended by two forts. Commander Rowan sent an expedition to capture them, which included the "Fanny," which was captured on October 1, 1861, while conveying men and stores to the Twentieth Indiana regiment, encamped at Chicamacomico, N. C., forty miles south of Hatteras Inlet. Sketch by W. T. Crane.

EVACUATION OF CORINTH.—General Halleck, with the grand army of the Tennessee, had steadily advanced the Federal army, after cutting Beauregard's railway communications to the north and east of Corinth. He expected to give battle on the 30th of May, 1862, but it was found that the Confederates had completed the evacuation of Corinth during the night, after firing the town at all important points and blowing up the magazines. The Federals pursued in the direction of Guntown, but only a few stragglers were captured. From a sketch by H. Lovie.

TROOPS IN READINESS TO QUELL EXPECTED RIOT IN BALTIMORE.—After the deplorable attack upon the Massachusetts regiment in Baltimore, General Banks caused the arrest of Marshall Kane and the police commissioners, which again aroused the mob so that a riot was imminent. In anticipation of attack Banks ordered Cook's Boston Light Infantry, supported by artillery, to take position in Monument Square, Baltimore, but the precaution was unnecessary. Sketch by Joseph Becker.

THE SURRENDER OF FORT PULASKI.—Fort Pulaski was built in 1829 for the defense of the Savannah River approach of Savannah, Ga. In January, 1861, it was seized by the authority of the State of Georgia, and subsequently turned over to the Confederate government. Its capture was determined upon after the taking of Port Royal, and an expedition was sent for that purpose. Batteries were erected by night under the command of General Gillmore, and the bombardment began on the 10th of April, 1861. By two o'clock a breach had been made which threatened the blowing up of the magazine, when the fort capitulated. From a sketch by W. T. Crane.

FEDERAL TROOPS LANDING OPPOSITE CAIRO, ILL.—After providing for the security of St. Louis, General Fremont turned his attention to the strengthening of Cairo, at the confluence of the Ohio and Mississippi Rivers, and sent a force to a point on the Kentucky shore for the purpose of building Fort Holt. From a sketch by Henry Lovie.

LANDING OF TROOPS AT FORT WALKER.—The authorities at Washington had decided that Port Royal, on the Coast of South Carolina, answered best the requirements for a naval rendezvous, and an expedition was fitted out on the 21st of October, 1861, which consisted of twenty-seven vessels under the command of Commodore Dupont. The largest fortification was Fort Walker, on Hilton Head, which was attacked early on November 7, 1861, and captured, when the transfer on shore was made of all the troops who had been spectators of the engagement. Sketched by W. T. Crane.

NORTH BATTERY OF THE CONFEDERATES AT SHIPPING POINT, looking up from the Potomac.—After the battle of First Bull Run the Confederates built batteries at all strategic points on the Potomac River.

SIEGE OF VICKSBURG.—Life in the trenches during the investment by the army under General Grant. In order to successfully accomplish the capture of Vicksburg, Grant proposed to attack from the south, and proceeded to dispose of the land forces to completely hem in all retreat. Expedition after expedition was organized, until all was ready on April 16th and Vicksburg was completely invested from the land side, while Porter's fleet commanded it from the river. On the 22d of May a simultaneous attack was made from both the land forces and the fleet, which was continued until the 6th of July, when a flag of truce was sent by General Pemberton, and the place capitulated. From a sketch by F. B Schell.

INTERIOR OF FLOATING BATTERY during the bombardment of Fort Sumter.—This novel battery performed a leading part in the attack on Fort Sumter. It was about one hundred feet long by twenty-five wide, built of sawed timber, presenting an angular front of about forty degrees. It was faced with two thicknesses of railroad iron, and was manned with four guns of heavy caliber.—Sketched by a Confederate officer.

GEN. HOOKER'S HEAD QUARTERS CHANCELLORVILLE MAY 1ST.

ATTACK ON GENERAL SEDGWICK'S CORPS.--CHANCELLORSVILLE. MAY 4, 1863.—Upon relieving Burnside, General Hooker reorganized the army and moved upon Lee's army, reaching Chancellorsville on the 30th of April Here he established his headquarters and sent out cavalry expeditions to cut Lee's railway communication with Richmond. General Sedgwick had been ordered to advance through Fredericksburg and unite with the main body at Chancellorsville, and made an unsuccessful attempt to pass around Early's left. Lee detached four brigades to intercept Sedgwick and an obstinate conflict followed. Sedgwick's force tried to overcome the attack, which was mainly directed against his left, but his efforts were futile, and he had finally to abandon the ground in a retreat toward Bank's Ford.—Sketched by Edwin Forbes.

98

RETURN OF FORAGING PARTIES.

FEDERAL ARMY ENTERING FRONT ROYAL after the battle of Winchester.—Jackson had been ordered to watch Banks and hold him while General Lee endeavored to cut off the Federal communication between Winchester and Alexandria. He pushed on to New Market, where he joined Elwell, to cut off at Front Royal Banks' possible retreat in that direction. The Federals were driven from their position and fell back to Front Royal.—Sketched by Edwin Forbes.

THE SIXTEENTH OHIO REGIMENT CROSSING TROY RUN VIADUCT.—After General McClellan had taken command at Grafton he decided upon an immediate advance upon the Confederate forces in Northwestern Virginia, and sent General Rosecrans to attack Pegram's position. The Sixteenth Ohio was sent forward by train on the Baltimore & Ohio Railroad.

VIEW OF FREDERICKSBURG, VA, from the North Bank of the Rappahannock River, after its Evacuation by the Confederate Troops.—Sketched by Edwin Forbes.

GENERAL KEYES' DIVISION CROSSING THE CHICKAHOMINY RIVER, MAY 23, 1862, over Bottom Bridge, built by the engineers of the Federal Army.—The Chickahominy forms the boundary between Henrico and Charles City Counties, Virginia, and was the theater of the operations of General McClellan against Richmond in May and June, 1862. Sketched by E. S. Hall.

EMBARKING TROOPS AT BIRD'S POINT, MO.—As soon as General Fremont established order in the Department of the West and organized an offensive movement against the Confederates below Cairo, he sent General Prentiss to occupy Cape Girardeon with a large force of artillery, cavalry and infantry, which landed at Bird's Point. Sketched by Henry Lovie.

RETREAT OF THE CONFEDERATES FROM CORINTH, MISS., and entry of the Federal Army.—The advance of General Halleck compelled the evacuation of Corinth by the Confederates, who departed by night after firing the town at all important places and blowing up the magazines. Sketched by Henry Lovie.

ON THE WAY TO THE FRONT.—Arrival and departure of the Federal soldiers at the Union Volunteer Refreshment Saloon, Philadelphia.—Sketched by F. B. Schell.

REFUGEES DRIVEN FROM THEIR HOMES by the Confederate General Von Dorn, after the battle of Pea Ridge. The Federal force under General Curtis was pushing southward to Fayetteville, which the Confederates had left burning before crossing the Boston Mountains.—Sketched by Henry Lovie.

CONFEDERATE ATTEMPT TO REGAIN THE WELDON RAILROAD.—During the operations around Petersburg, Warren took possession of the Weldon Railroad, where he strongly entrenched his line. Several attempts were made by the Confederates to recapture this position, but without success. The upper picture represents the Federal forces falling back through Charlestown, August 2, 1864.—Sketched by John Becker.

VIEW OF RICHMOND from the prison camp on Belle Isle, James River, just before the surrender.

108

THE ALABAMA ("290") hoisted the Confederate flag on August 24, 1862, and started on a cruise which lasted two years, and during which time she destroyed or captured over fifty vessels. On June 19, 1864, the United States steamer **Kearsarge,** Capt. John A. Winslow, destroyed the Alabama off Cherbourg, France.

BIRD'S-EYE VIEW OF CHATTANOOGA, TENN., as seen from Lookout Mountain.—Drawn by an engineer of General Bragg's staff.

VIEW OF THE CITY OF NEW BERNE, N. C., from the opposite bank of the Neuse River. The Tenth Connecticut Regiment awaiting transportation by the Flagship "Delaware," Commander Rowan.

FIVE LOCOMOTIVES BUILT AT VICKSBURG under the supervision of Colonel Colbough, of McPherson's staff.—Sketched by F. B. Schell.

CAPTUR... LOST MOUNTAIN BY GENERAL HOOKER, JUNE 15, 1864.—Sherman's army advanced in three columns toward Marietta, his object being to break the Confederate line between Kenesow and Pine Mountains. The Con-
...ates were so heavily pressed at all points that they soon had to adandon Lost Mountain as well as the long line of breastworks connecting it with Kenesow Mountain.—From a sketch by C. E. F. Hillen.

THE SIXTH MASSACHUSETTS REGIMENT LEAVING JERSEY CITY.—This was the first regiment to respond to the call of the President issued three days before. It was welcomed in New York with great enthusias and it was sped on its way with cheers of more than a hundred thousand spectators.—Sketched by A. Berghaus.

BATTLE OF WINCHESTER. Position of the Nineteenth Corps, General Emory in the center. September 19, 1864.—The Federal forces extended about four miles, enveloping Winchester from north and east. Sheridan formed a line of battle with the Sixth Corps. covered by Wilson's cavalry, the Ninteenth Corps in the centre. and the Konowha infantry on the right. 2. Early emerged from the hills west of Cedar Creek and struck the troop directly on Crook's right. Crook immediately charged with the entire Eighth Corps, but the whole Federal left and center became demoralized and were driven along the turnpike.—Sketched by J. E. Taylor.

115

EFFECT OF A DISCHARGE OF GRAPE ON GUNBOAT "IROQUOIS," killing eight and wounding seven of a gun crew of twenty-five men mounting a Dahlgren gun.—Sketched by Wm. Waud.

116

DEPOT OF ORDNANCE DEPARTMENT, at White House Landing, Pamunkey River, Va.—This place derived its name from a plain white wooden house, occupying the site of the residence of Mrs. Custis, afterwards the wife of Washington. The family of Lee had been residing at the White House, but had just before the arrival of the Federal troops removed to the neighborhood of Richmond.—Sketched by E. S. Hall.

FIRST OHIO REGIMENT SURPRISED BY A MASKED BATTERY.—Four companies were ordered to guard the railroad between Alexandria and Leesburg, and accompanied by Gen. R. C. Schenck were proceeding cautiously in cars and trucks pushed ahead of a locomotive. The train had just entered a deep cut when the cars were swept from front to rear by grape and canister. The troops leaped from the cars and rallied in the grove, maintaining so bold a front that the Confederates retired to Fairfax Court House.—Sketched by Henry Lovie.

ACCIDENT ON THE OHIO AND MISSISSIPPI RAILROAD.—It was remarkable how few accidents occurred upon railroads in the transportation of troops. Even when in the enemy's country and on their own ground hardly an accident is recorded except this, which makes it notable. The Nineteenth Illinois Regiment was on its way to the front when a bridge collapsed while the train was passing. The locomotive passed over safely, but the middle cars were precipitated into the creek, and over one hundred soldiers were killed and wounded.—Sketched by Henry Lovie.

DISTRIBUTING CAPTURED CLOTHING TO THE NEEDY. Headquarters of Vincent Collyer, Superintendent of the Poor.—After the capture of New Berne a large amount of clothing fell into the hands of the Federals, which was stored at this point, and headquarters established for its distribution among the needy inhabitants of New Berne and vicinity. It brought about much merry-making among the colored people.—Sketched by J. H. Schell.

THE "STEUBEN" REGIMENT RECEIVING ITS FLAGS.—The foreigners were among the first to respond to the call of the President. Col. John E. Bendix raised the famous German regiment, to which much attention was shown. Beautiful flags were made by ladies and presented with public ceremonies in front of the City Hall, New York, which greatly helped to stir the feeling of patriotism throughout the North. Colonel Bendix organized the Seventh New York regiment in 1861, and afterwards was promoted to brigadier-general in 1865.—A. Berghaus.

CAPTURE OF McCLERNAN'S HEADQUARTERS and McAllister's and Schwartz's artillery by the Confederates, April 6, 1862.—Grant's army lay at Pittsburg Landing awaiting the arrival of Buell from Nashville. His intention was to at once march upon Corinth. On Sunday, April 6, the Confederate army opposing him, under **Gen.** Albert Sidney Johnson, moved forward very quietly. and completely surprised the Federals. The onslaught was so fiercely made that three brigades were rapidly forced back, with the loss of a battery, upon McClernan's division, which lay in the rear of Prentiss's force. Prentiss was surrounded and surrendered, and the Confederates took possession of McClernan's camp and captured nearly half of both McAllister's and Schwartz's artillery, besides several of Dresser's cannons and a large number of horses.—Sketched by H. Lovie.

122

GENERAL McDOWELL'S ADVANCE along the new military road into Virginia.—Arrangements for an aggressive movement were finally completed on July 15, 1861, and on the afternoon of the next day all the divisions left camp and advanced toward Fairfax Court House, where it was expected the Confederates would make a stand.—Sketched by E. S. Hall.

DEPARTURE OF THE SEVENTH REGIMENT FROM NEW YORK.—This regiment, the just pride of New York city, and widely noted for its perfect discipline and equipment, as well as promptitude in every emergency, was the first regiment from the Empire State to respond to the call of the President. With bayonets gleaming in the sun, with firm step, with bearing proud and erect, they marched down Broadway, which was lined with people from sidewalk to roof. Two days later they were followed by the Sixth, the Twelfth and the Seventy-first.—Sketched by A. Berghaus.

THE SURPRISE AT PHILIPPI.—The Federal troops under command of Colonel Dumont, supported by Colonels Kelley and Lander, proceeded along the turnpike overlooking Philippi to surprise Colonel Porterfield's rear. After a march of thirteen miles in a drenching rainstorm, he was about taking position when Porterfield's pickets discovered the movement from a pistol shot fired by a woman at Colonel Lander, who was reconnoitering ahead of the column. Dumont opened fire with both guns and under this cover made a dash upon the enemy's picket and captured the barricaded bridge across the river.—Sketched by H. Lovie.

ELLSWORTH'S ZOUAVES.—The dashing exploits of the French Zouaves in the Crimean War attracted the emulative attention of all the light infantry tacticians of our country. A number of companies were formed, foremost of which was that of Ellsworth, who created a great sensation when he made a tour of the East with his Chicago cadets, with their striking and gay uniforms, with flowing pants, their jaunty crimson caps and open blue jackets. No military organization was more brilliant, and in their evolutions they displayed great precision.—Sketched by A. Berghaus.

LEW WALLACE'S CHARGE AT FORT DONELSON.—On February 11, 1862, General Grant decided to move upon Fort Donelson, which was situated on the left bank of the Cumberland River. The position was defended by General Floyd with 15,000 men. In the attack Colonel Wallace was ordered to capture a battery called the Middle Redoubt, and with three regiments he advanced rapidly up the hill until within forty rods of the battery, when a terrible fire from the entire line of opposing infantry, as well as artillery, compelled them to fall back. They were reinforced, but to no purpose, and after holding their ground for a full hour they fell back to their original position.—Sketched by Henry Lovie.

FORT HATTERAS, FROM RAMPARTS OF FORT CLARK.—In August, 1861, Commodore Stringham was informed that supplies for the Confederate troops were being carried through Hatteras Inlet, the entrance to Pamlico Sound, and a joint naval and military expedition was sent to capture Forts Clark and Hatteras, defending the inlet. The expedition landed on the 28th of August and mounted heavy guns, which opened upon the forts simultaneously with the squadron, when both forts surrendered without the loss of a man on the Union side.—Sketched by J. H. Schell.

ENGAGEMENT AT CULP'S HOUSE, GA., JUNE 22, 1864, which led up to the battle of Kenesaw Mountain, Ga., June 27, 1864.—Sherman was drawing his lines tightly around the Confederates, and on the 21st of June, 1864, Hood was ordered to take position on Hardee's left, at the same time Sherman was developing his right flank southward of Kenesaw Mountain. On the next day (22d) Hooker, having advanced his line, with Schofield on his right, was suddenly attacked by Hood near the Culp House, southwest of Marietta. His unexpected appearance and vigorous assault, which fell upon Williams' division of Hooker's corps and Hascall's division of Schofield's, drove both divisions back to the main line, where the Federal artillery checked their progress, when the advance of the whole Federal line drove Hood's forces back in confusion, with a loss of nearly 1,000 men. The Federal loss was 400 killed and wounded.—From a sketch by C. E. F. Hillen.

CAPE GIRARDEAU, MO., OCCUPIED BY THE FEDERAL TROOPS UNDER GEN. U. S. GRANT, SEPTEMBER 8, 1861, as a base of supplies for his proposed invasion of Kentucky.—When the Legislature of Kentucky met on September 5, 1861, the Governor in his message insisted on neutrality, and recommended that a State force be raised for its own defense and that all other military bodies should be disbanded. At the same time the Legislature was informed that Confederate troops occupied Hickman and Chalk Bluffs. General Polk also occupied Columbus. General Grant on the 7th took possession of Paducah, Ky., at the mouth of the Tennessee River, a few miles above Cairo, and made extensive preparations to resist the progress of Polk's army northward. Polk refused to withdraw with his troops when demanded to do so by the Kentucky Legislature unless Grant was made to also withdraw. This condition was considered as an insult to the dignity of the State, and the Legislature demanded an unconditional withdrawal and afterwards passed resolutions requesting Major Anderson to take command of the military forces of the State and repel the invasion of the Confederates.—From a sketch by Henry Lovie.

LANDING ON THE LEVEE, NEW ORLEANS, OF CAPTAIN BAILEY AND LIEUTENANT PERKINS WITH A FLAG OF TRUCE from General Butler, demanding the surrender of the city to the Federal forces.—On Friday, April 25, 1862, Farragut's fleet moved up the river and at noon came in full view of New Orleans, casting anchor an hour later, while a violent rain and thunder storm was prevailing. For five miles along the levee thousands of bales of cotton and barrels of sugar were burning, while in the stream were large ships, steamboats and smaller craft afire. The messengers with the flag of truce stepped ashore and proceeded to the City Hall through a motley crowd that kept up their cheers for Jefferson Davis and the Confederacy and groans and hisses for Abraham Lincoln and the Yankee fleet. General Lovell refused to surrender and advised Mayor Monroe not to allow the Confederate flags taken down. The messengers retired, and in the meantime some marines from the Pensacola hoisted the flag over the Mint, which was afterwards taken down, and the next day Captain Bell, with one hundred marines, raised the flag over the Custom House and Mint, and they were not afterwards disturbed. The city was peacefully occupied on the 30th of April, 1862.—From a sketch by Wm. Waud.

131

DRESS PARADE AND REVIEW OF THE FIRST SOUTH CAROLINA (COLORED) VOLUNTEERS, under Colonel Fessenden, U. S. A., at Hilton Head, S. C., June 25, 1862.—The organization of negro regiments was discoraged until after the failure of the campaign before Richmond. Congress, as the last important act of the session of 1862, empowered the President to "receive into the service of the United States for any military or naval service for which they may be found competent, persons of African descent, who shall be enrolled and organized under such regulations, not inconsistent with the constitution and the laws, as may be prescribed." It was further enacted that "any slave of a person in rebellion rendering such service shall forever thereafter be free together with his wife, mother and children if they also belong to persons in rebellion. The pay of these colored troops to be fixed at ten dollars a month and one ration."—From a sketch by W. T. Crane.

VIEW OF THE INTERIOR OF FORT BEAUREGARD ON BAY POINT, ST. PHILLIPS ISLAND, S. C., opposite Fort Walker, on Hilton Head, and commanding Port Royal Harbor.—On gaining possession of these forts, Beauregard was renamed Fort Seward and Walker Fort Miller.—General Sherman and Commander Dupont sailed for Fortress Monroe on October 29, 1862, on an expedition to gain possession of Port Royal Harbor, S. C. The fleet did not reach Port Royal bar until the 4th of November. The attack was further postponed until the 7th of November, owing to unfavorable weather. The forts had been hastily constructed and were not protected against shell or bombs. Fort Beauregard, the less elaborate, mounted fifteen guns with a battery of four guns behind an earthwork to the left. The Confederate forces were commanded by General Drayton. The Federal fleet received the fire of the batteries without reply, and then, when in favorable position, opened a fierce bombardment, which dismounted the guns and reduced the forts. The garrison took refuge in the woods and thus escaped. Forty-three guns were captured and possession gained of Hilton Head and Port Royal Harbor. Fort Beauregard was occupied for a time by the Sixty-ninth New York (Highlanders') Regiment.—From a sketch by W. T. Crane.

PLANTATION POLICE, OR HOME GUARD, examining passes on the road leading to the levee of the Mississippi River in the vicinity of Vicksburg, Miss., during its investment by the Federal Army.—With Grant's army commanding all the land approaches to Vicksburg, and the gunboats occupying the river, it became a matter of vital interest to the owners of the plantations that their slaves should be kept at home and not allowed to get within the Federal lines. This emergency called for the formation of a home guard and for a system of passes to prevent an exodus of the negro slaves. The night scene sketched by our artist shows the anxious care of the guard and the careless indifference of the negroes.—From a sketch by F. B. Schell.

PROVIDING BREAD FOR THE ARMY.   Great national bakery in the basement of the Capitol, Washington. D. C.—The exigencies of the time and the presence of a vast army in and around the National Capital made it necessary to improvise a bakeshop where thousands of loaves of bread could be provided daily. The Government selected the basement of the Capitol, where ovens were built, flour stored, and the whole process of breadmaking carried on. This furnishes one of the incidents of war times that gives an insight into the readiness with which the Government responded to every want of the soldier, and gave up even the great National Capitol to the use of supplying the daily bread needed by their gallant defenders.—From a sketch by A. Berghaus.

SECOND BATTLE OF BULL RUN, SATURDAY, AUGUST 30, 1862. The left of the Federal line of battle opposing the right wing and center of the Confederate army, commanded by Longstreet.—There had already been almost continuous fighting from the 26th, when Jackson passed through Thoroughfare Gap and reached Bristow Station. He had sent Stuart to capture Manassas Junction, which he accomplished that night and secured an immense quantity of commissary stores, ten locomotives and trains of quartermaster's supplies. The succeeding days, 27th, 28th, 29th, were days of sanguinary battle, and on the morning of the 30th a desperate battle was begun, which continued through the entire day, in which the entire available forces on both sides were brought into action. Pope could not hold out against the terrible onslaught of Lee's whole army, and he fell back behind Bull Run.—From a sketch by Edwin Forbes.

SECOND BATTLE OF BULL RUN, SATURDAY, AUGUST 30, 1862. The right wing of the Federal army opposing and attempting to turn the left of the Confederate forces, commanded by Jackson.— During the night of the 29th General Lee had made preparations for a general attack on Pope's front. He had drawn in Jackson's left, which was hidden from view by the intervening woods and hills, and posted forty-eight heavy guns in such a manner that he could sweep the ground to the right and left. Pope thought Jackson's army was retreating and hurried his right wing forward, hoping to turn Longstreet's left. As Porter's Corps advanced upon Jackson, the Confederates under Longstreet opened a terrible fire of shot and shell, enfilading Porter's ranks. Porter did not falter, but three times made vigorous attacks and made serious inroads upon Jackson, but each time was repulsed with great slaughter by the combined infantry and artillery fires. Finally he fell back to a defensive position until ordered to fall back by general orders from Pope.—From a sketch by Edwin Forbes

FORT PULASKI DURING THE SECOND DAY'S BOMBARDMENT, FRIDAY, APRIL 11, 1862.—This fort, situated on a mud island at the mouth of the Savannah River, commanded the approach of Savannah, Ga. General Gilmore had succeeded in planting eleven batteries, mounting thirty-six mortars and heavy guns, on shore, distant over one mile from the fort, and on the 16th of August demanded the surrender of the fort. This being refused by Commander Olmstead, fire was opened, and after eighteen hours the walls were thoroughly breached and the fort surrendered with forty-seven guns, a large amount of ammunition and nearly four hundred prisoners. The possession of the fort by the Federals barred all direct access to Savannah by sea, and the city became of no use to the Confederacy as a port of entry.—From a sketch by W. T. Crane.

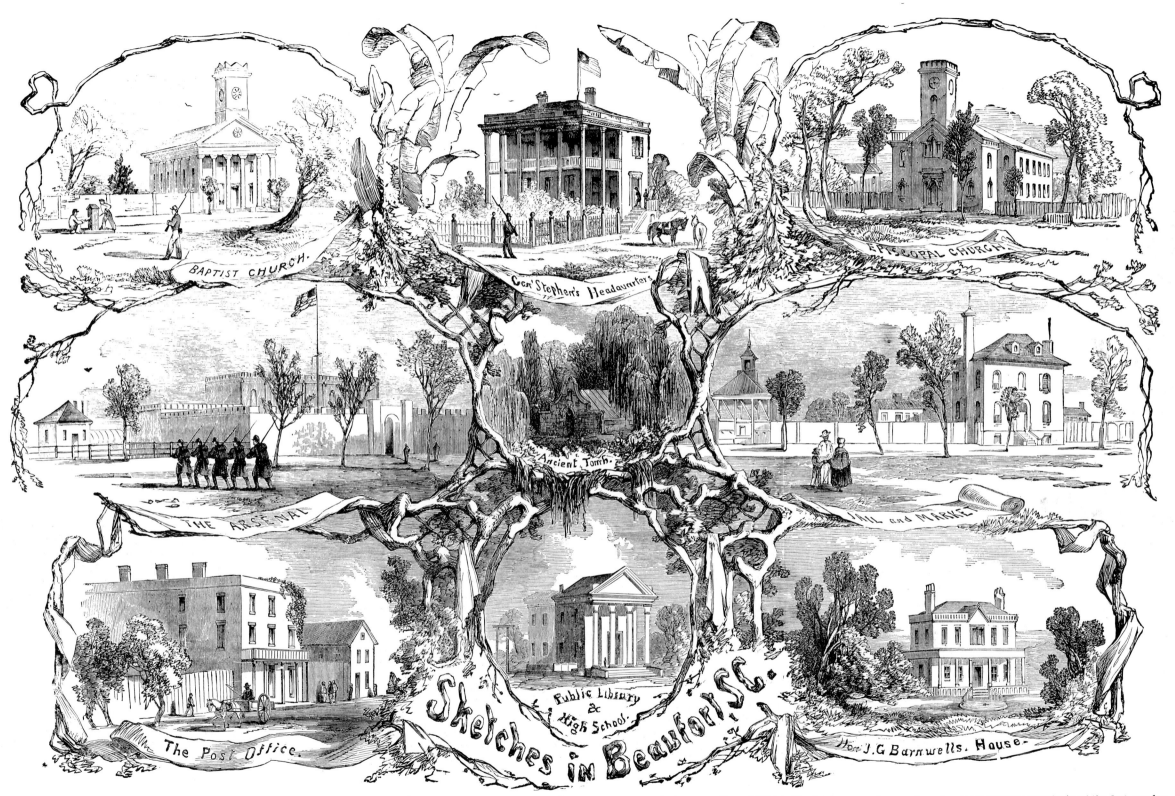

The sketch contains the following labels:

BAPTIST CHURCH.

Gen'l Stephen's Headquarters

EPISCOPAL CHURCH.

THE ARSENAL

Ancient Tomb.

JAIL and MARKET

The Post Office.

Public Library & High School.

Sketches in Beaufort, S.C.

Hon. J. G. Barnwell's House.

VIEWS IN BEAUFORT, S. C., Headquarters of the Department of the South.—After the reduction of Forts Beauregard and Walker and the occupation of Hilton Head, where a rendezvous for colored refugees was organized and the first regular colored regiment recruited, Gen. J. J. Stevens took possession of the old and aristocratic city of Beaufort, located on Port Royal Island and Port Royal river, on November 9, 1862. Here he established his headquarters, and as the harbor had nearly sixteen feet of water on the bar, it afforded an excellent port from which to direct future operations.—From a sketch by W. T. Crane.

PASSAGE OF THE SECOND DIVISION OF THE FEDERAL SQUADRON PAST FORTS JACKSON AND ST. PHILIP, APRIL 24, 1862.—Capt. Theodorus Bailey commanded this division and led it with the "Cayuga," as flag ship, followed by the "J. P. Jackson," "Pensacola," "Mississippi," "Portsmouth," "Oneida," "Katahdin," "Varuna," "Kineo," and "Wissahickon." As the "Cayuga" came on a line with Fort Jackson her battery opened a heavy fire, to which the "Cayuga" did not respond until close upon Fort St. Philip, when she opened upon the latter with grape and canister. The "Portsmouth" lost her tow, the "Jackson," and drifted down the river. The Confederate ram "Louisiana" and attending gunboats then attacked the "Cayuga," but Captain Bailey warded off the attempts of the ram, and the "Varuna" came to his rescue, although herself nearly hemmed in by the Confederate gunboats, and was afterwards severely rammed by the Geo. Moore and finally sunk just as she delivered a broadside of three guns.—From a sketch by Wm. Waud.

WOMEN'S MEETING AT COOPER UNION HALL, COOPER INSTITUTE, NEW YORK CITY., to organize the "Women's Central Association of Relief," for the comfort and aid of the sick and wounded defenders of the Federal cause—.This great meeting in New York city was the beginning of a great charity which cared for the sick and wounded and administered to the comfort and encouragement of the soldiers at the front. In the first three years of the war over one million of dollars were expended by the United States Sanitary Commission that sprang from this meeting, guided by the Rev. Dr. Henry W. Bellows. They supported over forty soldiers' homes, scattered over the whole field of war. Twenty-three hundred sick and wounded were daily ministered to in these homes. A hospital directory costing $20,000 per year was maintained, where friends could gain information of sick and wounded friends. From $3 to $10 was expended for the comfort of each wounded soldier after every great battle, and in every way the soldier's comfort studied and ministered.—From a sketch by A. Berghaus.

REVIEWING THE "CONTRABANDS" on their way to their day's work on the fortifications around Fortress Monroe.—General Butler, when he took command of Fortress Monroe, determined to use all the able bodied negroes who came into his camp at such work as had previously been done by the enlisted soldiers. This caused considerable discussion, and the claim made by General Butler that these fugitive slaves were "contraband of war" led to the general designation of the negro as "contraband." The sketch of our artist hardly needs comment, as it is a vivid interpreter of its own story.—From a sketch by W. T. Crane.

BATTLE OF PITTSBURG LANDING (SHILOH), SUNDAY, APRIL 6, 1862.—General Hulburt's division receiving the combined attack of Johnston, Chertham, Mithers and Breckenridge—Repulse of the Confederate forces at the Peach Orchard.—By noon the entire Federal advance had been driven in—routed for the most part—leaving three large encampments in the hands of the Confederates. Two divisions alone remained intact, Hurlbut's and W. H. L. Wallace's. These divisions protected the depots of ammunition and the transports. Hurlbut fell back to the patch of woods, abandoning his camp. Wallace soon after also fell back, crowding the remnant of the Federal army in a narrow semicircle extending half a mile from the landing. The battle had lasted for eight hours, and yet here stood Hurlbut bidding defiance to the victorious Confederates. The fire from twenty guns checked their advance. The two gunboats then took part; this new feature surprised he Confederates, they were compelled to withdraw from the field, and Beauregard made his night's camp at Shiloh church.—From a sketch by Henry Lovie.

DELAWARE INDIANS ACTING AS SCOUTS FOR THE FEDERAL ARMY IN THE WEST.—In 1789 there were within the limits of the United States, including the territories, less than 100,000 Indians. In 1853 the number had increased by acquisition of territory to more than 400,000. At the beginning of the Civil War all the great tribes had been driven west of the Mississippi. The Indian territory became an object of importance to Price and McCullough, and they found in some of the tribes possible reinforcements. Gen. Albert Pike was the commissioner of the Confederate States to the Indian nations and tribes west of Arkansas. In August, 1861, he entered into a treaty with the Comanches, promising them Confederate protection, giving their chief letters of safeguard. Other tribes followed, and with the exception of the Delawares, the more important tribes were induced to forsake their allegiance to the Federal Government. Thus the Confederacy hoped to secure their 52,000,000 acres of land.—From a sketch by A. Berghaus.

EXPLOSION OF THE MINE BEFORE PETERSBURG.—Beauregard had made the place almost impregnable, and after various attacks Grant, becoming convinced that capture by assault was impossible, began the erection of intrenchments to lay siege to the place.   General Burnside, with a regiment of Schuylkill miners, constructed a mine extending from his rifle pits, 170 yards, to a point within the Confederate lines, with lateral galleries extending 37 feet right and left.   Upon the exploding of the mine the Ninth Corps Artillery (in the fore ground), to silence the enemy's batteries not affected by the explosion, made a charge.   The fort was found to have been converted into a yawning crater, burying guns and men, and dividing Elliott's brigade, which was panic stricken.   The Federals swarmed in and beyond the crater, subjected all the while to the concentrated fire of all the batteries, while Beauregard rallied his men and, after one of the bloodiest hand to hand conflicts of the war, finally drove the Federal forces back.   The loss on both sides was frightful, and the affair was characterized as most discreditable to the National Armies.—Sketched by Andrew McCallum.

GENERAL ROSSER ENDEAVORING TO SAVE HIS LAST GUN.—General Sheridan was selected as best fitted to carry out a dashing, aggressive campaign against Early and Fitzhugh Lee, who were continually making raids into Pennsylvania, and with 40,000 men advanced upon Winchester. He sent two divisions of cavalry to take New Market, twenty miles in Early's rear. General Rosser made an ineffectual effort to intercept him, but was defeated and suffered heavy loss. The illustration shows his desperate effort to save his last gun.—Sketched by J. E. Taylor.

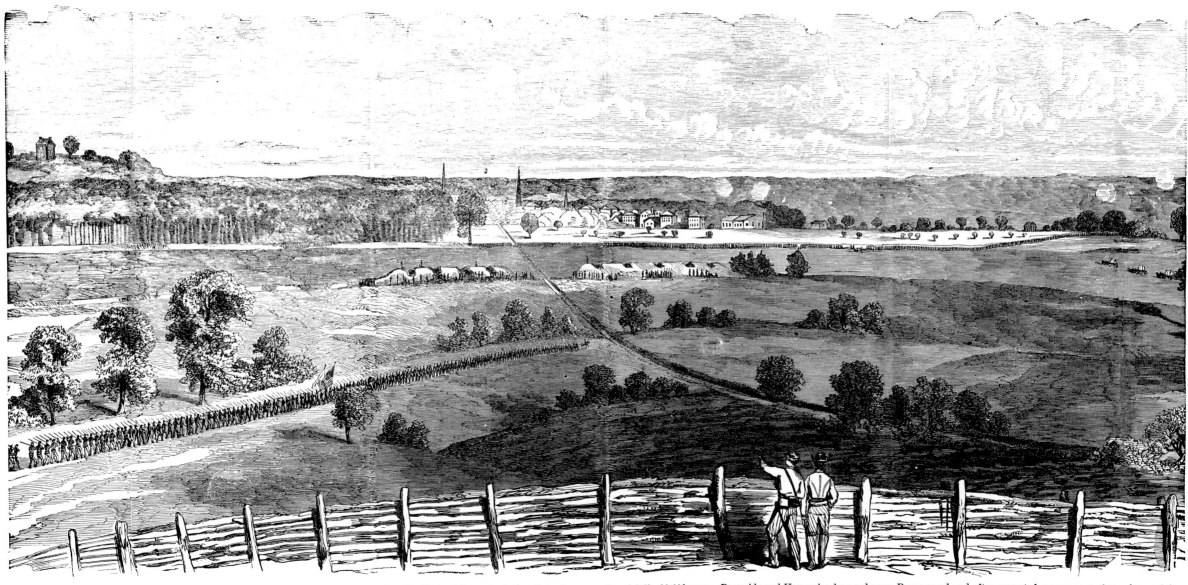

ADVANCE OF THE FEDERAL ARMY AGAINST PETERSBURG.—The Federal forces besieging Petersburg numbered fully 90,000 men. Burnside and Hancock advanced upon Beauregard and after repeated successes and repulses established a footing and forced the Confederates to retire to an inner line of defense, which was done in the face of an enemy numbering ten to one, and which proved almost impregnable. The same line further strengthened repelled the continuous assaults of the Federal army until evacuated at the close of the war.—Sketched by Edwin Forbes.

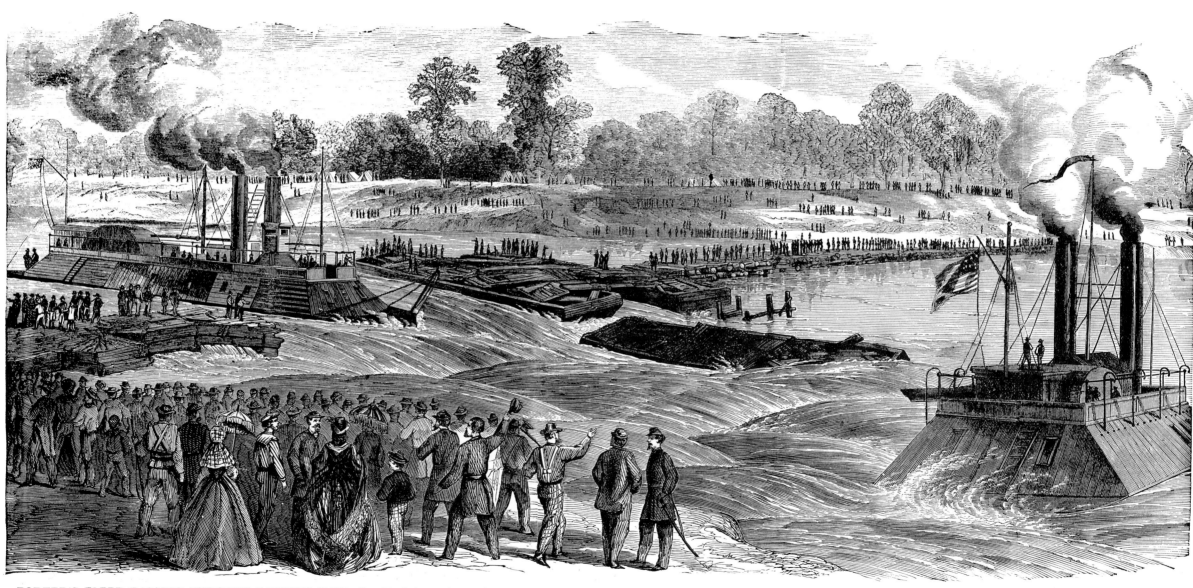

PORTER'S FLEET PASSING THROUGH BAILEY'S DAM.—Grant had given orders to close up the campaign on Red River, but Admiral Porter found that the river had fallen so much that he could not get his vessels over the rapids above Alexandria ; but Lieutenant Colonel Bailey of the Fourth Wisconsin Volunteers constructed a large dam, which raised the water high enough to admit the passage of the entire fleet. It took two days to raise the water sufficiently to allow his largest vessels to pass through safely   For this brilliant service Bailey received the thanks of Congress and was made brigadier-general of Volunteers.   Porter re-entered the Mississippi with his fleet, where he remained until relieved during the ensuing Summer.—Sketched by C. E H. Bonwill.

THE BATTLE OF COLD HARBOR. The Eighteenth Corps driving Longstreet's forces from their first line of rifle pits.—Sheridan's cavalry had seized Cold Harbor. General Smith had moved a force of 16,000 men down the James River to co-operate with General Wright. Lee, being kept informed of this movement, had sent Longstreet to the same cross roads, where Smith and Wright found him strongly intrenched. They gave battle and drove him beyond Cold Harbor to a second line of trenches. The advance was made over an open field in the face of a galling fire and was brilliant in the extreme, though the loss on the Federal side was very heavy, 2000 men having fallen in that short engagement.—Sketched by Edwin Forbes.

BATTLE AT BETHESDA CHURCH, MAY 30, 1864.—There are two roads leading from Hanover Town direct to Richmond ; these Lee defended with his entire force.   His position could not be broken, so Grant moved across the Tolopotomoy
Creek.   Lee did the same, and both armies were now on their old ground.   The Confederates threatened to turn Warren's left by a move on Mechanicsville, but General Crawford brought up the reserves to cover the road.   Reaching Bethesda
Church, a division of Ewell's corps charged them furiously on the flank.   General Crawford brought up the remainder of the reserves and with the support of Col. Kitching's brigade repulsed the attack.—Sketched by Edwin Forbes.

THE BATTLE OF THE WILDERNESS, MAY 5, 1864.—Gen. Grant, upon assuming the supreme command, reserved for himself the special field of Virginia. His objective was Lee's army defending Richmond, and his design was to turn
Lee's right. He sent 100,000 men across the Rapidan and marched through the Wilderness due south, camping the next day close to the enemy. Lee attempted to turn Grant's left and throw him back upon the river. The battle began at
5 o'clock in the morning, when Hancock fell upon Hill and drove him a mile down the Plankroad. While rearranging his troops Longstreet suddenly attacked him, and he was driven back to his old lines. In the afternoon Lee again attacked
Hancock, but nothing decisive was accomplished, although the Federal loss amounted to 15,000 men.—Sketched by J. Becker.

THE BATTLE OF SPOTTSYLVANIA COURT HOUSE.—General Grant endeavored to plant his army between Lee and Richmond by a movement upon Spottsylvania Court House, fifteen miles south-east of the battle-field of the Wilderness. Warren's forces were to take the advance, with Hancock and Burnside to follow, and when the withdrawal of trains apprised Lee that some movement was being made, but not knowing the objective, he instructed Longstreet's Corps to move out of their breastworks and camp in readiness to move to Spottsylvania Court House in the morning. Not finding a place to bivouac, he began the march that night. In consequence of this night march, Lee was able to place himself in Grant's path, and on the following morning the Army of the Potomac filed into line in front of Lee's position. The scene represents Burnside and Hancock engaging the enemy. Various movements were made from flank to flank, and every assault was repulsed.—Sketched by J. Becker.

THE BATTLE OF GAINES' MILLS, JUNE 27, 1862.—After the Battle of Mechanicsville McClellan learned that Jackson had crossed Beaver Dam Creek, and he saw that Lee intended to cut off the Federals from their base of supplies at the White House. The stores and ammunition were ordered removed to Savage's Station, and by daylight the troops and nearly all the heavy guns had crossed the New Bridge and were at Gaines' Mills. The Confederates advanced under Hill, who was reinforced later by Longstreet and Jackson, driving the Federals through the swamp. The whole line was so fiercely attacked that it could make no stand until Richardson's two brigades with Sike's division checked the advance by rapidly marching through the lines and making a bold stand, while the retreating columns were being reformed. The remaining batteries were soon again directed upon the pursuers, and the Confederate attack was repulsed. During the ensuing night the Federals crossed the Chickahominy and burned all the bridges.—Sketched by Wm. Waud.

BATTLE OF WILLIS CHURCH, JUNE 30, 1862.—As soon as it was ascertained that the Federals were in retreat after the battle of Gaines' mills, Jackson, Longstreet and Hill were ordered to cross the Chickahominy and attack the retreating army. The Federals, after crossing White Oak Creek, formed a new line at Willis Church, Hancock's forces being on the right, while Porter occupied the left, with Heintzelman and Sumner in the center. Jackson opened on Hancock's troops and attempted to rebuild the bridge which checked his advance. Longstreet and Hill now came up, and the conflict became severe. Point after point was vainly tried in the determined effort to break the Federal line. Finally a general onslaught was made and after severe hand to hand conflict the Confederates retired. During the ensuing night the Federals moved to Malvern Hill.—Sketched by an officer on Heintzelman's staff.

VIEW OF CASTLE PINCKNEY.—Upon Major Anderson's transfer to Fort Sumter the Convention of South Carolina at once requested Governor Pickens to take possession of Forts Moultrie, Johnson and Castle Pinckney. Colonel Pettigrew immediately seized Castle Pinckney, Lieutenant Mead having fled with his troops to Sumter. His men barricaded the door, spiked the guns, ruined the carriages and removed all the ammunition amid the cheers of thousands on the shore. Pettigrew unfurled the Palmetto Flag, which was the first flag raised over a national fortification.

FEDERAL ARTILLERY TAKING POSITION.—Sketched by F. H. Schell.

OPENING OF THE BATTLE OF ANTIETAM.—Hooker's division fording Antietam Creek to attack the Confederates. The Federal army, which had fallen back from Chantilly to the fortifications around Washington, was reorganized by General McClellan, who had been raised to the supreme command of the defenses of Washington. Lee with D. H. Hill determined upon an immediate invasion of Maryland. He captured Harper's Ferry, but being in a dangerous position, withdrew. McClellan immediately ordered pursuit.

BATTLE AT JERICHO FORD, MAY 23, 1864.—General Hancock, withdrawing the Second Corps under cover of the remaining troops, headed southward. Lee, during this flank movement, sent Longstreet on a parallel road in the direction taken by Hancock and also sent Ewell to follow Longstreet. When the Army of the Potomac reached North Anna Creek the Army of Northern Virginia was there to receive them, having taken a shorter route. The battle lasted all day with varying success. Toward evening a determined onslaught placed the Federal flag in the enemy's redan, and the following morning the Confederates abandoned their works.—Sketched by Edwin Forbes.

BATTLE OF THE WILDERNESS, MAY 6, 1864.—The forces under General Grant found themselves face to face with the entire Confederate army under General Lee, and the attack was made along the whole line.—Sketched by J. Becker.

167

BATTLE OF SPOTTSYLVANIA COURT HOUSE.—In the movement of General Grant to throw his army between Lee's forces and Richmond General Warren, with the Fifth Corps, was to take the advance. Hancock was to follow, while Sedgwick and Burnside were to move by an exterior route. When he emerged from the woods into a clearing two miles north of Spottsylvania Court House, he came upon Longstreet's Corps, which had arrived at the same place, but fearing to engage with his small number, he waited for Sedgwick before making an attack. They lay down under cover of any ridge or projection which offered and waited for reinforcements.—Sketched by Edwin Forbes.

BATTLE OF THE WILDERNESS.—The whole of Grant's army found themselves opposed to General Lee. The illustration shows the general advance of Hancock's forces, which occupied the extreme right.—Sketched by J. Becker.

CITIZENS OF ATLANTA LEAVING THE CITY.—When General Sherman took possession of Atlanta his troops were given a period of rest. On the 8th of September General Sherman himself rode into Atlanta. He immediately determined to convert the city into a purely military station, and ordered the citizens to leave. A tart correspondence took place between General Hood and himself against this course, but Sherman was immovable, and some 1,700 persons were sent back into the Confederacy.

ATTACK ON CONFEDERATE BATTERIES ON KENESAW MOUNTAIN.—General Johnston formed his line extending on the crest of Kenesaw Mountain. Sherman extended his right and began the attack with the Fifteenth Army Corps as shown in the illustration.—Sketched by J. F. E. Hillen.

159

WAGON TRAIN PASSING THROUGH RESACA AT NIGHT.—General Sherman had organized a magnificent force for his campaign in Georgia. It required 100 locomotives and 1,000 cars to transport supplies. He began the campaign with nearly 100,000 men and 250 cannon, comprising the army of the Cumberland, Major-General Thomas; army of the Tennessee, Major-General McPherson, and army of the Ohio, Major-General Schofield. The Cavalry numbered over 12,000 men. McPherson made a rapid march by night to cut Johnston's communications at Resaca.

ATTACK ON KENESAW MOUNTAIN.—Sherman's right consisted of the Seventeenth Corps, which began the attack upon General Johnston, whose line extended over the crest of the Mountain.—Sketched by J. F. E Hillen.

160

THE EVACUATION OF FORT MOULTRIE BY MAJOR ANDERSON.—With the promulgation of the Ordinance of Secession in South Carolina, open intimations were given out that unless the forts were speedily surrendered they would be occupied by force. Major Anderson, in command, was instructed from Washington to avoid every act that would needlessly tend to provoke aggression, but to hold possession of the forts in the harbor, and if attacked to defend himself to the last extremity. Major Anderson, recognizing the weakness of Fort Moultrie and the hopelessness of resistance in case Sumter was occupied, transferred his little command to Fort Sumter on the night of December 20, 1862, the very night the Commissioners arrived in Washington to demand the surrender of the forts. In evacuating Fort Moultrie he spiked the guns, destroyed the carriages and carried off all the available munitions.

"STAR OF THE WEST" APPROACHING SUMTER.—Public sentiment in the North demanded some action on the part of the Government toward the relief of Major Anderson and his little band locked up in Fort Sumter, and in conformity with the demand the "Star of the West," loaded with supplies, was dispatched from New York. When opposite Morris Island she was fired into from the batteries on the Island and compelled to return to New York. Major Anderson then wrote to Governor Pickens, asking if the firing upon an unarmed vessel carrying the flag of the Government was authorized by him. Governor Pickens replied, "The act is perfectly justified by me."

DEPARTURE FROM NEW YORK OF THE ELLSWORTH ZOUAVES.—When volunteers were called for Ellsworth resigned his commission in the army, went to New York, and from the firemen of that city organized a regiment who, accustomed to hard work and extreme vigilance, proved excellent material for active service, especially under the peculiar drill and discipline adopted by Colonel Ellsworth. This regiment was known as the New York Fire Zouaves, and upon their departure for Washington on the 24th of May, 1862, they were escorted to the wharf by the New York Fire Department and created a deep impression upon the city.

ENCAMPMENT OF THE ELLSWORTH FIRE ZOUAVES.—The regiment arrived in Washington May 24, 1862, and went into camp at Alexandria, Va. Before going into camp and while engaged in destroying means of communication southward by railroad and telegraph, Colonel Ellsworth, accompanied by a small guard, caught sight of a Confederate flag flying from the Marshall House. He entered the house, secured the flag, and on his way down was shot down by the proprietor, J. W. Jackson. One of his guards immediately shot Jackson through the head and thrust his bayonet through the body before it had fallen from the step.

THE BATTLE AT RAPPAHANNOCK CROSSING, VA., NOVEMBER 7, 1863.—A portion of General Sedgwick's corps and skirmishers of Forty-fourth New York Regiment charging the Confederate works. In Meade's Virginia campaign, when Lee was at Culpepper, General Sedgwick crossed the Rappahannock and gained the rear of Early's force, where they were opened upon with a lively fire. A storming party formed of Upton's and Russell's brigades carried the works by assault, capturing 1,500 prisoners. This advantage was not followed up, and Lee availed himself of the opportunity to withdraw to the Rapidan.—Sketched by Edwin Forbes.

THE ARMY OF THE POTOMAC CROSSING JAMES RIVER, at Donthard's, on a pontoon bridge constructed by General Benham, June 14, 1864. General Grant having determined to change his base, transferred the army by a flank movement to the south side of the James River. At the point selected the channel was thirteen fathoms deep, and the pontoon bridge had to be floated to cover two thousand feet. The first section was launched during the forenoon, and the entire bridge was completed before midnight.—Sketched by Edwin Forbes.

THE FORTS AND BREASTWORKS NEAR PETERSBURG, captured by the Eighteenth Corps under Gen. W. F. Smith, June 15, 1864. Butler determined to make another effort to capture Petersburg, and ordered Smith to move against the city. He advanced with such force that Beauregard withdrew from his intrenchments. He had just completed a battery of heavy guns from Richmond, which his chief engineer also advised him to evacuate. The guns were dismounted and with the carriages and chassis were carefully buried in the vicinity of the battery, so well concealing the spot that the Federals failed to discover them. When Pickett's division recovered the position on the 18th everything was recovered, mounted and used.—Sketched by Edwin Forbes.

BATTLE OF FISHER'S HILL, SEPTEMBER 23, 1864, BETWEEN SHERIDAN AND EARLY.—After the battle of Winchester Early retreated to Fisher's Hill. Sheridan arrived in front of this position on the 22d of June and made ready for a direct attack. This was ineffectual, and a general advance broke Early's line and he retired in confusion, leaving several hundred prisoners and sixteen pieces of artillery in the hands of Sheridan. Early was not prepared for this attack, and but for the checking of Forbert's flank movement with a small Confederate cavalry force, it is acknowledged that Sheridan would have annihilated him. As it was Early lost half his army and retreated to the lower passes of the Blue Ridge.—Sketched by J. E. Taylor.

GENERAL CROOK'S CHARGE AT FISHER'S HILL, SEPTEMBER 23, 1864.—Sheridan sent two divisions of cavalry under Torbert by the Luray Valley to gain New Market, twenty miles in Early's rear. A cavalry dash was made for the right, under cover of which Crook's corps of infantry moved to that flank and carried the Confederate left on North Mountain. This charge was executed with great dash and contributed largely to the success of the day.—Sketched by J. E. Taylor.

THE BURNING OF THE "HARVEY BIRCH," an American merchantman, while on her way from Havre to New York.—She was brought to by a shot from the Confederate privateer "Nashville," and was then boarded by a Confederate officer and a boat's crew, who took Captain Nelson and his men as prisoners, carried away all that was valuable, and then set fire to her, causing the entire destruction of a vessel valued at $150,000. The "Nashville" was of 1,100 tons burden and 800 horse-power, and carried two twelve-pound rifled guns.

THE "MISSISSIPPI" FIRING ON A CONFEDERATE STEAMER.—As soon as Butler had raised and equipped a volunteer force for Southern waters he established a rendezvous at Ship Island, off the Mississippi Coast, as the best point within striking distance of every important locality of the Gulf of Mexico.

COL. LEWIS WALLACE AND HIS STAFF of the Eleventh Indiana Regiment was placed in command of Fort Henry while Grant commenced his preparations for the advance on Fort Donalson.

171

BURNING A CONFEDERATE SCHOONER by a detachment of the Potomac Flotilla under Lieutenant Howell.—After the battle of Bull Run the War Department sent forces to police the Potomac to prevent ravages being made by the Confederates. A detachment found a schooner laden with supplies and burned it.

STATION HOUSE CELL, WASHINGTON, D. C.—After the appointment of General Porter as provost-marshal he found so much demoralization and dissipation among the officers and men that the morale of the army was fast declining. He established rigid discipline, and the city resumed its usual quiet.

172

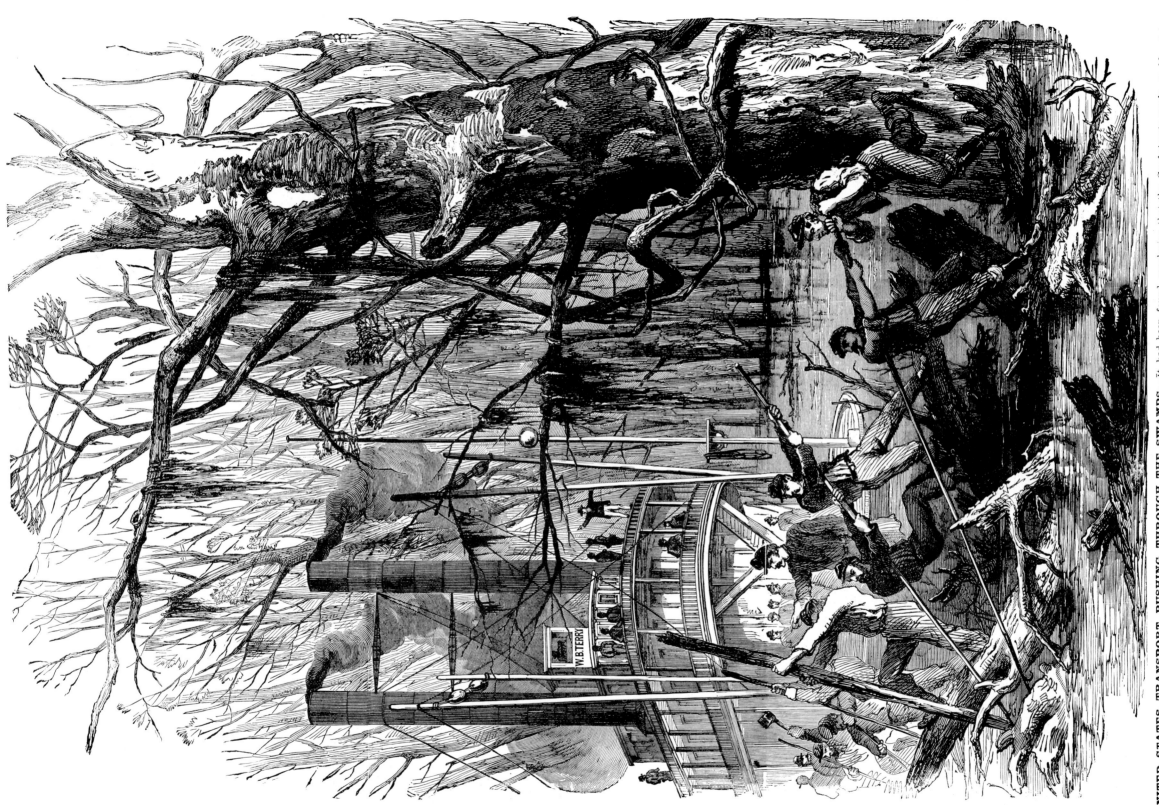

UNITED STATES TRANSPORT PUSHING THROUGH THE SWAMPS.—It had been found conclusive that the Confederate works could not be captured by the fleet alone, and that a land force should be in position to co-operate effectively by attacking the rear. Pope had come to a like conclusion and sent three steamboats from Cairo, and a canal was begun which should admit of the transportation of the troops. This was done by cutting through irregular bayous and thick timber.—Sketched by H. Lovie.

173

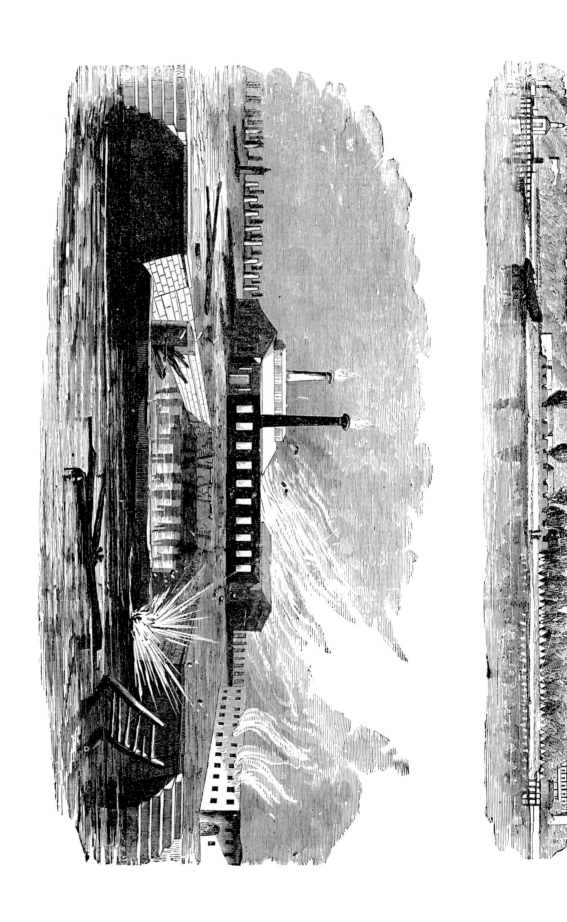

BURNING OF THE NORFOLK NAVY YARD.

NAVAL HOSPITAL AND BATTERY AT PORTSMOUTH, VA.

REMOVING SUNKEN SCHOONERS WHICH BLOCKADED THE ENTRANCE OF THE JAMES RIVER.

174

THIRTEEN-INCH MORTAR used by the Federals. Weight, 17,000 pounds.
RECRUITING IN PHILADELPHIA for the famous Bucktail Regiment.

BAGGAGE TRAIN ON THE MARCH.—General Pope ordered all available forces to concentrate at Manassas Junction, but it was impossible for them to be carried out literally, for the distance was great along a wooded road, intersected by a great number of streams and marshy lands, and encumbered by thousands of wagons belonging to Pope's army. The illustration represents the condition of the roads and the enormous difficulty of moving heavy trains.—Sketched by Edwin Forbes.

BATTLE OF PLEASANT HILL, LA., APRIL 9, 1864.—After the disastrous battle of Sabine Cross Roads on the 8th, the Thirteenth Corps and Lee's Cavalry had fallen back in a disorganized mass, when General Emory's division of the Nineteenth Corps came up, meeting the fugitives three miles back of where the battle had been fought, closely followed by the victorious enemy. The division made a stand with fixed bayonets and repulsed the Confederates, who retired to Mansfield. It was then decided by Banks to retreat to Pleasant Hill. Emory's division brought up the rear of the retreating army, burying the dead and bringing off the wounded. Gen. Kirby Smith had orderek Taylor to follow up Banks' army, and in order to save the fleet in the river Banks was obliged to make a stand, although he had less than 15,000 men, consisting of the Nineteenth Corps and the Western troops under A. J. Smith. The Federals held rising ground, and presented a stubborn front to every attack. After a stubborn contest Smith's reserves were brought up, and the Confederates retreated. There being no water or food at Pleasant Hill, Banks fell back to Grand Ecore, where he could communicate with Porter's fleet.—From a sketch by C. E. H. Bonwill.

THE ARMY OF GEN. JOSEPH HOOKER ON THE MARCH TO THE BATTLEFIELD OF CHANCELLORSVILLE, VA., APRIL 28, 1863.—In January, 1863, General Hooker assumed command of the Army of the Potomac. He employed the next three months in repairing the demoralized condition of the army, and when he determined to move upon Lee he had an effective and well equipped army of 132,000 men. General Lee had about 60,000 men encamped on the southern bank of the Rappahannock River, his right extending to Port Royal and his left to about two miles above Fredericksburg. General Hooker's plan of attack was as follows : Three corps were to be massed two miles below Fredericksburg to cross there and make a bold feint, two of the corps to immediately return and join Hooker ; in the meantime the remaining four corps were to cross above Fredericksburg. Our artist has caught a glimpse of the army as it was marching to its position, and made from it a characteristic sketch of army life.—From a sketch by Edwin Forbes.

ENGAGAGEMENT AT ROMNEY, VA., JUNE 11, 1861.—The Eleventh Indiana Zouaves, Col. Lewis Wallace, crossing the bridge over the Potomac river on the double quick. At Romney, the county seat of Hampshire County, Va., about fifty miles southeast of Cumberland, a large Confederate force had concentrated early in June, 1861, and Colonel Wallace, of the Eleventh Indiana Regiment stationed at Cumberland, hearing of this movement, determined to move against it. He proceeded twenty-eight miles by railroad to New Creek bridge and then marched twenty-two miles to Romney, reaching there at eight o'clock on the morning of the 11th of June. The Confederate force of about 1,200 men, learning through scouts of the advance, made but feeble resistance and fled in wild disorder, followed by the Zouaves at "double quick." They were in time to partake of the breakfast prepared for the Confederate soldiers and captured one office and several tents, etc.—From a sketch by Henry Lovie.

VIEW OF GRAFTON, VA., ON THE MONONGAHELA RIVER—HEADQUARTERS OF GENERAL GEORGE B. McCLELLAN, IN JUNE, 1861.—This beautiful little town is situated on the banks of the Monongahela River, ninety-six miles below Wheeling, one hundred and ninety from Pittsburg, and two hundred and seventy-nine miles from Baltimore. In June, 1861, General McClellan, while operating in West Virginia, established his headquarters at Grafton. Our sketch was made at the time of Lieutenant Tompkins' return there with his gallant Company B, U. S. Dragoons, after their dashing raid into Fairfax Court House, on June 1, 1861, in the face of fifteen hundred Confederate troops.—From a sketch by Henry Lovie.

BOMBARDMENT OF FORT SUMTER, APRIL, 1861. SKETCHED FROM MORRIS ISLAND, CHARLESTON HARBOR.—For nearly four months Major Anderson and his little band of fifty-five artillerists, nine officers, 15 musicians and thirty laborers had been holding the fort, awaiting the action of the Federal Government to either order its evacuation or to furnish them needed supplies. In the meantime the State of South Carolina had taken possession of Fort Moultrie, unspiked the guns left maimed by Major Anderson, added others, and greatly strengthened the fort. They had as well constructed a floating battery, fortified Cummings' Point and erected on it an iron-clad battery and erected a battery on Morris Island. When the first gun was fired upon Sumter all these batteries opened upon the fort, which finally resulted in its capture.—From a sketch by a Confederate officer.

INTERIOR OF FORT THOMPSON, N. C., AFTER ITS CAPTURE BY THE FEDERAL FORCES—VIEW OF NEW BERNE IN THE DISTANCE—BURNING OF ROSIN WORKS, RAILWAY BRIDGE AND NAVAL STORES BY THE RETREATING CONFEDERATES.—After the capture of Roanoke Island General Burnside directed its force in conjunction with the naval division against New Berne. The two commands embarked from Hatteras Inlet, March 12, 1862, and that night anchored off Slocum's Creek, eighteen miles below New Berne. Here the next morning the military division landed under cover of the fleet and took up their march along the railroad and turnpike. The Confederate works were five miles below New Berne and a mile in extent, and defended by eight regiments of infantry, five hundred cavalry and three batteries of six guns each, commanded by General Bruch. After four hours' fighting the fort was abandoned and the Confederates took up their retreat to New Berne, the three brigades of Burnside in full pursuit. In the meantime the gunboats came up, a steamer was captured and the troops conveyed down the river, and the Confederates escaped by railroad to Goldsboro.—From a sketch by F. B. Schell.

THE CAPTURE OF THE UNITED STATES GUNBOATS "CLIFTON" AND "SACHEM" IN THEIR ATTACK ON SABINE PASS, SEPTEMBER 8, 1863.—An expedition sailed from New Orleans September 5, 1863, under Gen. W. B. Franklin, with a military force of five thousand men of the Nineteenth Corps and four light-draft gunboats, the "Clifton," "Aragona," "Sachem" and "Granite City," under Lieutenant Crocker. The aim of the expedition was to secure Sabine City, at the mouth of the Sabine River. The pass was strongly protected by two thirty-four pounders, a battery of field pieces and two boats converted into rams. The Federal gunboats were simply ferry-boats and merchant vessels lightly built and not calculated to encounter heavy guns from a fort. The forts withheld their fire until the gunboats were clean abreast, when they opened fire from eight guns. The "Clifton" and "Sachem" each ran aground under the enemy's guns and were disabled and obliged to surrender. It was then found that the Confederate garrison consisted of but forty-seven men. The "Aragona" and "Granite City" escaped, and the expedition proved a failure.—From a sketch by an officer.

SKIRMISHING BETWEEN SHARPSHOOTERS ON PICKET DUTY IN THE OPPOSING ARMIES IN VIRGINIA EARLY IN THE WAR.—As the two armies lay in their trenches during the long periods of preparation, the monotony was frequently broken by a sharp exchange of rifle balls between the opposing pickets. This led to various devices to draw the fire of the other by presenting a cap on a rail, which, when it exposed the marksman, made him a ready target to the wily sharpshooter.

THE UNITED STATES MILITARY TELEGRAPH.—The illustration represents a station of the Military Telegraph. As the army advanced, it was accompanied by a corps of men belonging exclusively to the Telegraph Bureau, who made all the necessary wire connections for the prompt transmission of orders between the General Commanding and the War Department. The operator is here seen at his night work, receiving dispatches, while a mounted orderly is waiting in order to convey them to the division generals. The Military Telegraph played an important part in the conduct of the several campaigns, and was perfected so as to become indispensable to the War Department in directing operations, although some of the Federal generals who gained success in the West claimed that their success was due to the fact that they were not in telegraphic communication with Washington, and the only use of the line was to announce their victory.—From sketches by Joseph Becker.

184

A NORTHERN EDITOR TARRED AND FEATHERED FOR PUBLISHING DISLOYAL EXPRESSIONS OF SYMPATHY FOR THE SOUTHERN CAUSE.—The scene of this outburst of popular indignation is but a single example of the feeling that pervaded the North against the people of the South. When war was declared and the opposing armies were in the field, the spirit of brotherly love was entirely overshadowed by that of hate, and to express sympathy or even pity for the enemy was deemed on either side disloyalty.

PRACTICING WITH THE CELEBRATED SAWYER GUN ON THE CONFEDERATE BATTERIES AT SEWALL'S POINT, NEAR NORFOLK, VA., from Fort Calhoun, on the riprap in front of Fortress Monroe. The distance was three and one-half miles, the guns were forty-two pounders (rifle), columbiads, and were the only guns then in use that could carry that distance. They made fearful havoc with the iron-clad batteries on the Point, three and one-half miles distant.—From a sketch by F. B. Schell.

185

REVIEW OF CONFEDERATE TROOPS EN ROUTE TO VIRGINIA, AS THEY PASS THE PULASKI MONUMENT, SAVANNAH, GA., AUGUST 7, 1861.—The same "pomp and glory of war" is exhibited in this sketch of the review of a Confederate regiment as it starts out to do service for the cause of its State, as is in other pictures of Federal troops as they march through the streets of New York to join issue with the Southern foe.—From a sketch by a refugee.

ENCAMPMENT OF FEDERAL TROOPS ON THE BATTERY OF ANNAPOLIS, MD., IN 1861.—The first troops from the North to reach the National Capital were sent by way of Annapolis, Md., on account of the destruction of the railroad bridges between Baltimore and Washington, and the Seventh New York Regiment was one of the early ones to take this route.—From a sketch by a volunteer.

186

THE "QUAKER CITY," IN LYNN HAVEN BAY, NEAR CAPE HENRY, VA.—The "Quaker City," Commander Carr, one of the United States flotilla of the Potomac, while cruising in Lynn Haven Bay, near Cape Henry, picked up a refugee from Norfolk, named Lynch, who represented that the master plumber of the Norfolk Navy Yard was ashore, and wished to be taken off.

AN ENGINE OF DESTRUCTION.—A machine designed to blow up the "Pawnee" and other vessels of the Potomac flotilla was set adrift near Aquia Creek. It was picked up while floating toward the "Pawnee." It was constituted of two large eighty-gallon oil casks, acting as buoys, connected by twenty-five fathoms of three-and-a-half-inch rope, buoyed with large squares of cork, every two feet secured to casks by iron handles. A heavy bomb of boiler iron, fitted with a brass tap, and filled with powder, was suspended to the casks six feet under water. It was intended by the contrivers of this weapon of warfare that the shock of a collision should light the fuse, explode the charge and blow up any craft with which it came in contact.

HOISTING THE FEDERAL ENSIGN ON THE STATE CAPITOL, BATON ROUGE, LA., MAY 7, 1862.—Officer Parker, of the United States gunboat "Essex," on the occupation of the city by General Gowen's troops, carried the Federal ensign to the flagstaff of the capitol and raised it to the breeze amid the cheers of the soldiers.

SCENE ON THE LEVEE, BATON ROUGE, LA. UNLOADING MILITARY STORES FOR THE FEDERAL TROOPS FROM THE TRANS-PORT "NORTH STAR," OVER THE MISSISSIPPI STEAMBOAT "IBERVILLE."—The city was occupied by a small force under Gen. Thomas Williams, and on August 5, 1862, was attacked by a Confederate force of five thousand troops under General Breckinridge, and after a contest of two hours, in which General Williams was killed, the Confederates were repulsed.—From a sketch by William Waud.

188

A FLOATING HOSPITAL—CONVEYING WOUNDED SOLDIERS ON A RAFT AFTER THE BATTLE OF BAYOU TECHE, LA., JANUARY 15, 1863.—The Confederate steamer "J. A. Cotton" had committed depredations along the Bayou Teche, and General Banks advanced with four gunboats and six infantry and one cavalry regiments up the Bayou to capture the vessel. They encountered earthworks, under whose guns the steamer lay. The troops attacked the batteries from the rear and the gunboats from the water, and forced the "Cotton" to retire towards an upper battery. Commander Buchanan of the Federal fleet was killed.

PLANTING THE STARS AND STRIPES ON THE CONFEDERATE FORT HINDMAN, AFTER THE BATTLE OF ARKANSAS POST, ARK., JANUARY 11, 1863.—Gen. C. G. Burbridge, accompanied by his staff, mounts the parapet and unfurls the flag. The place was attacked by the combined military and naval forces, under McClernand and Porter, and the works carried by storm. A large number of prisoners were captured with quantities of stores.—From sketch by W. R. McComas.

189

SCENE ON THE HURRICANE DECK OF THE "NORTH STAR."—Soldiers of the Forty-first Massachusetts, writing home, on their arrival off Ship Island. The soldiers, 15,000 strong, under General Butler, had taken passage at Fortress Monroe and were sent in detachments to some point unknown to them in the South. They had a long and stormy voyage and finally arrived at Ship Island, where they found a strong naval force under Farragut, and they were to capture New Orleans by way of the Mississippi River. After so much uncertainty, both to themselves and their friends at home, they hurriedly notified their friends of their whereabouts and possible destination.

ADVANCE UPON PORT HUDSON, LA.—Baggage train of General Augur's Division crossing Bayou Montecino, March 13, 1863. General Banks, with an army of 25,000 men, made a strong demonstration against Port Hudson, on the 13th, intended as a diversion in favor of Admiral Farragut, who was to run the batteries. The naval undertaking was unsuccessful, and General Banks only had a slight encounter with the enemy and returned his army to Baton Rouge.—Sketched by F. H. Schell.

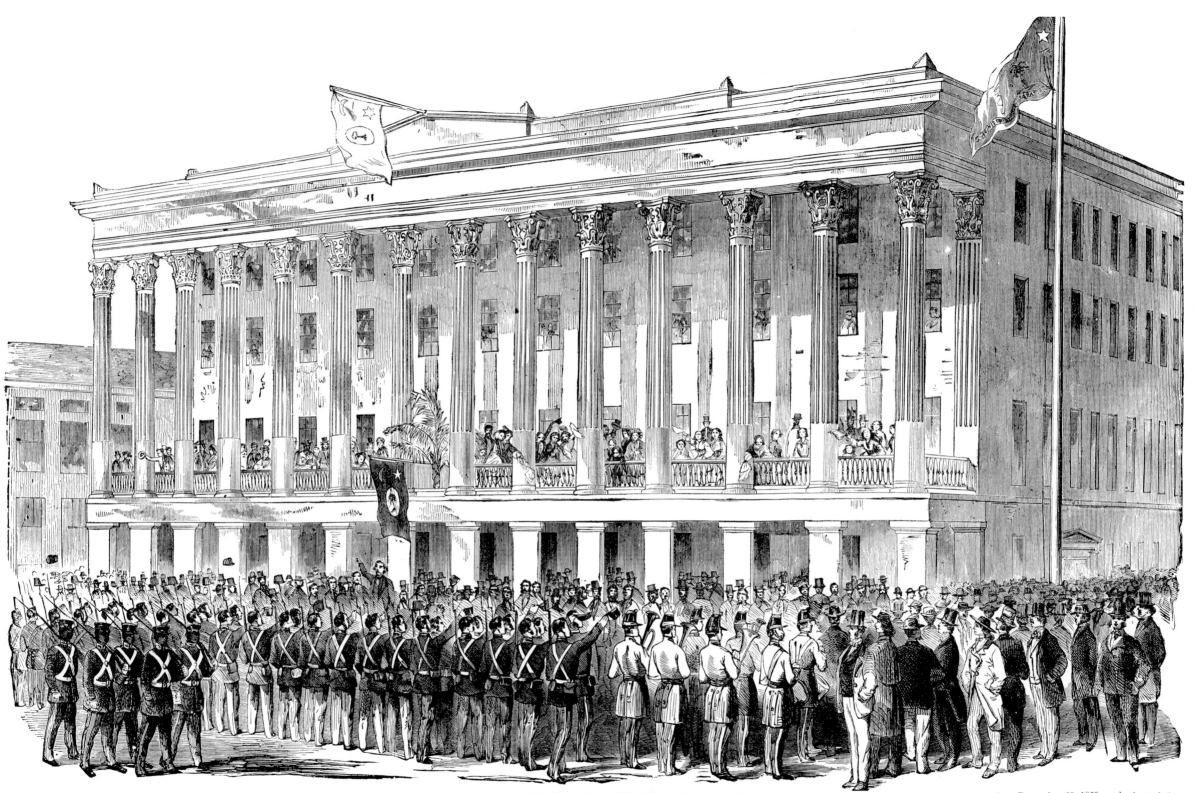

THE ABBEVILLE VOLUNTEERS IN FRONT OF THE CHARLESTON HOTEL, CHARLESTON, S. C., DECEMBER 22, 1860.—The State of South Carolina passed an ordinance of secession, December 20, 1860, and adopted the State flag as the highest evidence of allegiance and at once seized all the arsenals and other United States property within its borders, substituting the Palmetto flag for the Stars and Stripes. The State militia was called out to take possession of the property and defend the State as a free and independent sovereign against the United States or any antagonistic independent State. The Abbeville Guard, the crack regiment of the State, was among the first of the armed forces to reach Charleston to take part in the reduction of Fort Sumter, the only United States fort in the State that refused to surrender.

THE FIRST CONVENTION OF DELEGATES FROM THE SECEDING STATES, organized February 4, 1861, with Howell Cobb as president.—This convention in a four days' session named themselves "The Confederate States of America," adopted a constitution and provided a provisional government, of which Jefferson Davis was chosen president and Alexander H. Stevens vice-president. This convention was held in the State House at Montgomery, Alabama, which upon the inauguration of President Davis, on February 18, 1861, became the capital of the Confederate States.

RE-ENLISTMENT OF THE SEVENTEENTH ARMY CORPS.—This corps was commanded by Major-General J. B. McPherson, who was appointed to the command on the 18th of December, 1862. It was organized from troops taken from General Grant, and when the period of enlistment expired, the whole corps re-enlisted with great enthusiasm.—Sketched by Henry Lovie.

COLLISION BETWEEN CONFEDERATE SCHOONER AND FEDERAL TRANSPORT.—The transport "Chi-Kiong" was laden with troops for the Southern campaign, and was proceeding South when it came in collision with a schooner, which was probably intentionally placed in her path.—Sketched by an Officer.

DISCOVERY OF UNBURIED FEDERAL DEAD.—During Meade's Campaign in Virginia, when he was falling back upon Centreville, a portion of his force, in crossing the old battlefield of Groveton, which was fought August 28, 29 and 30, 1862, came upon piles of Federal dead which had remained unburied. The battle of Groveton was fought between Pope, McDowell and Hooker on the Federal side, and Jackson and Longstreet on the Confederate side, with great loss on both sides, and resulted in a defeat for the Federal arms.—Sketched by Edwin Forbes.

BATTLE OF PEA RIDGE, MO., MARCH 7, 1862.—The Federal Forces under Generals Curtis, Siegel and Asboth; the Confederate army commanded by Generals Von Dorn, Price and McCulloch. The Federal army was actively on its way southward from Springfield, Mo., in hopes of meeting General Price. General Von Dorn advanced with Price and arrived at Pea Ridge, or Elk Horn, as it was called by the Confederates, and immediately began the attack. The cavalry and a battery were sent ahead and had apparently dispersed the force in front, but when the main body of Federals came up the woods were found to be full of Confederates, who fell upon the advancing force and made such a fierce onslaught upon it that it was broken asunder and almost swept from the field, with the loss of two of its guns. The illustration represents the beginning of the attack.—Sketched by a Federal Officer.

BATTERY OF PARROTT GUNS OPPOSITE EDWARD'S FERRY, OCTOBER 22, 1861.—After the battle of Bull Run, General Gorman was ordered to make a feint from Edward's Ferry. Colonel Dana was sent with two companies under cover of guns from Rickett's battery. They came upon a Confederate regiment and had a skirmish in the woods. Suddenly they were attacked by a force of two regiments and a body of cavalry and were forced to fall back. Upon hearing the firing Colonel Baker with the California Regiment was sent from Harrison's Island, and took command of the entire force, which numbered 1,900 men. The Confederates meanwhile had collected their forces, and the fight became general. The Federals advanced in the face of a terrific fire pouring upon them from all sides, but at the very outset Colonel Baker fell dead, pierced by bullets in head, side and arm.—Sketched by F. B. Schell.

RETREAT ACROSS CANAL BOAT BRIDGE AT EDWARD'S FERRY, OCTOBER 23, 1861.—The battle described on the preceding page was waged with great fierceness. Colonel Cogswell took Baker's place, and being sorely pressed, decided, as evening was coming on, to cut his way through to Edward's Ferry. As this was being done the ammunition gave out and the retreat became a rout. Meanwhile General Stone crossed with 2,500 of Gorman's brigade, but was soon met by fugitives who reported the Confederates as advancing in great force. Nothing was to be done but retreat, which was done successfully across the canal-boat bridge, and hold Harrison's Island until the arrival of reinforcements.—Sketched by F. B. Schell.

TAKING FORMAL POSSESSION OF VICKSBURG, ON JULY 4, 1863.—The terms of capitulation having been arranged on the third of July, 1863, at ten o'clock, the following morning Pemberton's entire force had stacked arms in front of the works under guard of McPherson's corps. The Federal force, under General Grant, then entered and took formal possession, capturing 27,000 officers and men as prisoners, 128 pieces of artillery, 80 siege guns, arms and ammunition for fully 60,000 men, besides an immense quantity of property such as cars, railroad equipments, steamboats, cotton, etc. Vicksburg was afterwards occupied by the divisions of Generals Logan, Herron and Smith. As a result of this capitulation Port Hudson was surrendered to General Banks on the 9th.—Sketched by F. B. Schell.

BOMBARDMENT OF FORT HINDMAN.—This fortification, commonly known as Arkansas Post, was located on the north bank of the Arkansas River, 170 miles below Little Rock. Sherman and Porter matured a plan for its capture and on the 10th of January, 1863, landed a force of 25,000 men three miles below the place. The gunboats accompanying the expedition opened upon the fort and continued a fierce bombardment until dark, while the Fifteenth Corps advanced toward the rear of the works, and the Thirteenth took position on the extreme left. The next day the gunboats and field batteries opened fire, and the Federals advanced upon the double quick. General Morgan's force carried the rifle pits and scaled the parapets on the eastern side, while Sherman took possession of the northern side. The Confederates at once hoisted the white flag and surrendered possession of the entire fort and all its approaches.—Sketched by W. R. McComas.

FARRAGUT'S FLEET BEFORE PORT HUDSON.—On the night of May 23, 1862, Banks crossed the Mississippi and invested Port Hudson, with the co-operation of Generals Auger and Sherman. Farragut was stationed above Port Hudson with the "Hartford" and the "Albatross" and several smaller vessels. The gun and mortar boats kept up such a steady bombardment that the first Confederate line had to be abandoned. A general assault was ordered, but after repeated charges it only resulted in driving the Confederates into their fortifications, but still maintaining their ground. The left was repulsed and had to fall back with great loss.—Sketched by F. B. Schell.

ASSAULT ON PORT HUDSON.—Following the operations described in the preceding page, a second assault was made, June 11, 1863. The Federals succeeded in reaching the parapets, but in attempting to scale them they were repulsed by a terrible fire. Again and again the troops charged upon the fortifications, and hand to hand encounters stubbornly contested the ground. By means of mining the Federal lines were brought nearer, and upon the news of the surrender of Vicksburg General Gardner sent a flag of truce and arranged terms for the capitulation of the place, which was completed on the 9th of July. The Federals captured 445 officers and 6,500 men, together with much property.—Sketched by F. B. Schell.

BURNING OF THE PENITENTIARY AT MILLEDGEVILLE, GA.—The Legislature of Georgia was in session at Milledgeville when Sherman started for Atlanta, but adjourned for dinner upon the news of Sherman's approach and did not return. The penitentiary convicts were organized into a company under Dr. Roberts, a felon, and did good service. The penitentiary was set on fire and much property destroyed.

CONFEDERATE PRISONERS TAKING UP TORPEDOES.—General Hazen's division was sent against Fort McAllister, which is sixteen miles from Savannah, on the Great Ogeechee River. It is an earthwork commanding the river which the Confederates had protected by planting branches of live oaks and torpedoes in front of the works. After the capture, General Sherman ordered these torpedoes to be removed by the Confederate prisoners themselves.— Sketched by James E. Taylor.

GENERAL GEARY ISSUING PASSES TO THE CITIZENS OF SAVANNAH.—General Sherman telegraphed to President Lincoln the capture of Savannah as a Christmas gift. He obtained 250 siege guns, 31,000 bales of cotton and a vast quantity of stores. The citizens he allowed to depart as they wished.—Sketched by J. E. Taylor.

RECEPTION OF GENERAL SHERMAN ON BOARD THE "NEMAHA."—General Sherman watched the storming of the fort (described in the preceding illustration), and, with characteristic impatience, he incurred every peril and in the night, in an open boat, picked his way through forest and river to find the commander of the fleet. The illustration shows him seeking news.—Sketched by J. E. Taylor.

AN INCIDENT OF BATTLE.—A faithful dog watching by the dead body of his master.

A BAGGAGE TRAIN CROSSING THE MOUNTAINS IN A STORM.—Sketched by C. E. F. Hillen.

STORMING A FORT BEFORE PETERSBURG.—Smith's Eighteenth Corps making the assault upon the fort at the right of the Confederate line. For three hours the whole strength of the Federal force was directed upon this point, and a lodgment was finally effected. During this movement the Twenty-second Regiment distinguished itself by a brilliant attack, carrying the first line of the Confederate works, and opening the way for a permanent foothold.—Sketched by Edwin Forbes.

Portraits of the Colonels of the Veteran Regiments who Re-enlisted for the War.
Lt.-Col. R. Avery, 102d N. Y.
Col. G. L. Prescott, 32d Mass.

Col. O. H Morris, 66th N. Y.
Lt.-Col. J. McConihe, 169th N. Y.

Col. W. Krzyzanowski, 58th N. Y.
Col. P. Kelly, 88th N. Y.

207

The capture of Buzzard's Roost at Honey Gap, Ga.—Sketched by J. E. Taylor.

205

Ruins of a Confederate Fort at Atlanta.

General Geary's Headquarters at Atlanta.

The City Hall, Atlanta.

BATTLE OF ANTIETAM CREEK, MD., SEPTEMBER 17, 1862.—Burnside's division on the left wing of McClellan's army. The charge of Hawkins' Zouaves, Colonel Kimball, on the Confederate battery on the hill. This battle was known by the Confederate Army as the Battle of Sharpsburg. On the extreme left Burnside had made two unsuccessful attempts to cross the Antietam Creek. At three o'clock in the afternoon he, at the head of his division, drove the enemy back until checked by a row of hills occupied by batteries. The Zouaves charged and captured the first battery. A. P. Hill's division then arrived, and Burnside's demand for reinforcements not being met, he fell back to the bridge, which the Confederates did not venture to attack.—From a sketch by Edwin Forbes.

RECEPTION OF COL. MICHAEL CORCORAN BY THE MAYOR AND CITIZENS OF NEW YORK CITY, AUGUST 22, 1862, on his release from the Confederate prison in which he had been confined for one year a prisoner of war.—General Corcoran was born in Ireland, September 21, 1827, emigrated to America in 1849 and settled in New York city. He was colonel of the Sixty-ninth Regiment, N. Y. S. M., and at the outbreak of the Civil War led it to the front and took part in the first battle of Bull Run, where he was taken prisoner and confined in the Confederate prison at Richmond, Va., and afterwards at Charleston, S. C. On being exchanged he returned to New York city and organized the Corcoran Legion and was made Brigadier-General of volunteers, and while in service was thrown from his horse and fatally injured. He died at Fairfax Court House, Va., December 22, 1863.—From a sketch by A. Berghaus.

DESPERATE NAVAL COMBAT BETWEEN THE CONFEDERATE IRONCLAD RAM "ARKANSAS" AND THE FEDERAL GUN-BOAT "CARONDELET," AT THE MOUTH OF THE YAZOO RIVER, JULY 15, 1862.—Second only to the memorable conflict between the "Merrimac" and "Monitor," on Hampton Roads, was this naval duel. The "Carondelet," commanded by Captain Walker, was sent by Admiral Farragut to locate the new Confederate iron-plated ram "Arkansas," reported to be a monster of tremendous power. On the morning of the 15th, after steaming up the Yazoo River about fifteen miles, the "Tyler," a consort, was ahead and suddenly received a shot, which passed over her. A broadside from the "Tyler" did not apparently affect the ironclad, but her shot disabled the "Tyler," while the bow-guns of the "Carondelet," directed against her antagonist, had no perceptible effect, while the "Arkansas'" shot pierced the "Carondelet." Then Captain Walker determined to board the enemy, which he did, but found the enemy safely locked inside their iron-proof shell, meanwhile pouring shot, shell, hot water and musket and pistol shots on the crew of the "Carondelet," which finally ran aground, and the "Arkansas" drifted down to encounter the Federal fleet, already warned by the "Tyler" of her presence. She escaped from all and gained the protection of the Confederate batteries below.—From a sketch by Captain Walker.

211

BURNING OF THE WHITE HOUSE, VA.—The Army of the Potomac abandoning their position on the Pamunkey River. Departure of the Federal flotilla for the James. On May 16, 1862, General McClellan, on his advance up the Peninsula, established his headquarters at the White House. This place is thirty miles north of Williamsburg and twenty-five miles east of Richmond, with which it is connected by the Richmond and York River railroads. It takes its name from a small wooden house painted white, which was the home of Mrs. Martha Custis when she married George Washington, and at the time of its occupation by McClellan had been deserted by the Lee family, who inherited it from George Washington Custis, through his daughter, the wife of Robert E. Lee, just before the advent of the Federal Army. On McClellan changing his base to the James River this place was burned, June 28, 1862, and the same day taken possession of by Stewart's Confederate cavalry.—From a sketch by William Waud.

212

BATTLE OF CROSS KEYS, VA., JUNE 8, 1862.—Stonewall Jackson was being pursued up the valley by the forces under Fremont, Ewell's division making a feigned attack on Harper's Ferry on May 29th. Jackson continued the next day pushing his reunited force towards Strasburg. Fremont was at Wardersville, on the other side of the mountain. He passed through Brent's Gap and his advance came upon Jackson's rear, who got clear to Strasburg. At Mt. Jackson the Confederates crossed the river and burned the bridge just as the Federals appeared on the opposite bank. The repairing of the bridge gave Jackson a day's start, and he reached Harrisonburg on the 5th. From here he turned east towards Port Republic, hoping to cross the river before Shields could come up. Colonel Wyndham, of the Federal cavalry, made a reconnoissance on the 7th, fell into ambush, and was captured with a considerable body of cavalrymen. In this engagement Ashby was killed. On the 8th Fremont attacked the forces under Ewell, who was posted at Cross Keys, midway between Harrisonburg and Port Republic. Jackson was near Port Republic, four miles further up the valley, and here was opposed by Shields. Fremont brought about 9,000 men against Ewell, who had 6,000. The battle lasted all day, when Ewell was ordered to join Jackson.—From a sketch by Edwin Forbes.

BATTLE OF PORT REPUBLIC, VA., JUNE 9, 1862.—After the battle of Cross Keys, when Ewell had been ordered to join Jackson, who was with his army at Port Republic, confronted by the Federal division under General Shields, General Fremont did not at once take up his march in the wake of Ewell's march, but remained for the entire day at Cross Keys. Shields had reached Port Republic on the 8th. A body of cavalry dashed across the river into the town and planted a gun opposite the entrance to the bridge. A Confederate brigade drove them back and captured the gun. Ewell, on the morning of the 9th, crossed the river, burned the bridge and placed the river between himself and Fremont. Shields repelled the repeated assaults of the Confederates until a Confederate brigade, marching through a dense forest, charged upon the left flank, commanded by Tyler, forced his position, captured his guns and caused him to retreat, followed for four miles by the pursuing enemy. At the close of the battle Fremont first appeared on the opposite bank of the river, but did not attempt to cross. Here ended the pursuit of Jackson.—From a sketch by Edwin Forbes.

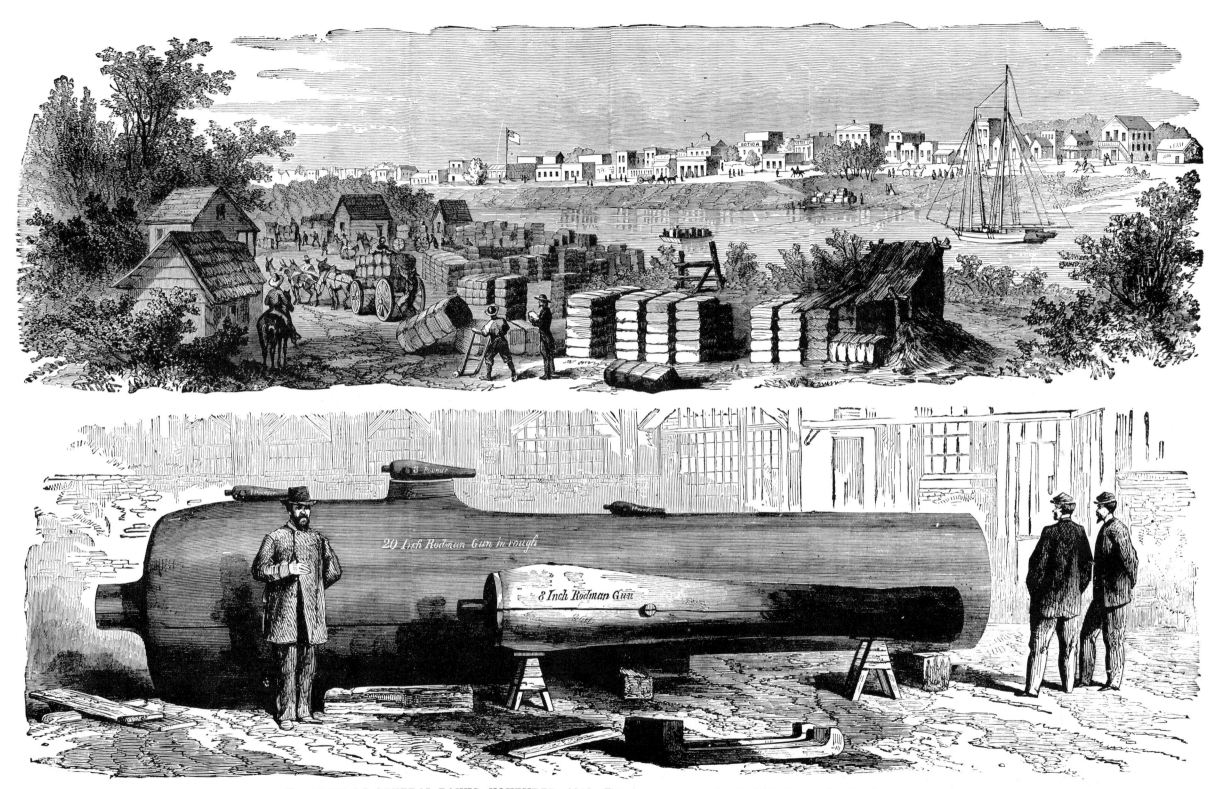

BROWNSVILLE, TEXAS, OCCUPIED BY THE ARMY OF GENERAL BANKS, NOVEMBER, 1863.—This river port is situated on the left bank of the Rio Grande, opposite Matamoros (Mexico), about forty miles from the mouth of the river. It was captured from the Confederates by General Banks in November, 1863.—From a sketch by L. Avery.

A TWENTY-INCH RODMAN GUN.—Mammoth cannon cast at Fort Pitt Foundry, in 1863. Gen. Thomas J. Rodman, of the U. S. Army, devised the method of casting cannon and shell on a hollow core, kept cool by a stream of water. He also invented a form of Columbiad, known as the Rodman gun, the largest of which was cast at Fort Pitt, in 1863, and had a twenty-inch bore. Many thirteen and fifteen-inch Rodman guns were used during the war for monitors and in forts.—From a photograph.

HEADQUARTERS OF GENERAL BUTTERFIELD, NEAR HARRISON'S LANDING, JAMES RIVER, VA.

FEDERAL PICKET BOAT, NEAR FERNANDINA, FLORIDA, attacked by Confederate Sharpshooters in the trees on the banks.

FEDERAL TROOPS MARCHING THROUGH THE STREETS OF FERNANDINA, FLORIDA.

216

PRESIDENT LINCOLN REVIEWING THE ARMY OF GENERAL McCLELLAN AT HARRISON'S LANDING, JULY 8, 1862.—The two opposing armies had been fighting before Richmond from June 26 to July 1, 1862. McClellan had fallen back to Harrison's Landing. He had lost in the seven days' battles 1,582 killed, 7,809 wounded, 5,958 missing, a total of 15,249. The Confederates had met with a loss fully as great. The question as to reinforcing McClellan's depleted army and continuing the campaign against Richmond by way of the Peninsula, or withdrawing it as advised by Pope, who had assumed command of the Army of Virginia, had determined the President to visit McClellan and review his army. Our artist has made a sketch of this review.—From a sketch by Edwin Forbes.

THE SOLDIER IN THE SUTLER'S STORE, is a sketch that tells its own story and needs no comment. It is evidently pay-day and the sutler is making hay while the sun shines.

VIEW OF SAVANNAH, GA., LOOKING EAST TOWARDS FORT JACKSON.—This view was sketched from the tower of the Exchange by W. T. Crane and gives the appearance of the city as presented when occupied by the Federal troops, in December, 1864, and presented as a Christmas gift by General Sherman to the National Union. Savannah was one of the few Southern cities not burned upon its evacuation. With the exception of some cotton and naval stores fired in the streets none of its property was destroyed, and its streets were peaceably occupied by the soldiers, who had just completed their march through Georgia.

SCENE OF THE FIGHT BETWEEN DETACHMENTS OF THE SIXTH CORPS AND GORDON'S DIVISION OF EWELL'S CORPS, FORT STEVENS, WASHINGTON, D. C., JULY 12, 1864.—In the latter days of June, 1864, General Early was ordered to move down the valley of the Shenandoah with his force of scarcely 20,000 men. The Federal force was equally small, as the bulk of the army was with Grant between Washington and Richmond. Early moved his force with rapidity, making fully twenty miles per day. He reached Maryland Heights, cut the Chesapeake Canal and tore up the Baltimore & Ohio Railroad for miles. Nothing prevented his marching into Pennsylvania, or Maryland, or even on Washington. On July 9th Early came upon Wallace at the Monocacy, and the Federal forces retreated in good order towards Baltimore. The approach to Washington was now fully open, and Early with 10,000 men marched upon the National Capitol. Had he marched with his usual celerity he could have taken possession of the city with but little resistance. On the evening of the 10th Early was within six miles of the Capitol. On the evening of the 12th he advanced his lines clear up to Fort Stevens. During the previous night the Nineteenth Corps and two divisions of the Sixth Corps had landed at the Potomac wharf. Towards the evening of the 12th a brigade of the Sixth Corps moved out to dislodge the Confederates, who had kept up an annoying demonstration on Fort Stevens. Each side lost heavily. The troops of Early were driven from the field and his opportunity was past.—From a sketch by A. Berghaus.

GENERAL BUTLER'S ARMY IN CAMP SOUTH OF THE JAMES RIVER, VA.—The troops in position awaiting an attack from Beauregard. The Army of the James, on May 4, 1864, changed their base from the York to the James River, and on May 5th landed on the south side of the James at City Point, Fort Powhattan and Bermuda Hundred. The army, by order of General Grant, then entrenched and constructed a defensive front across the narrow neck of Bermuda Hundred, and within three miles of the Richmond & Petersburg Railroad, which Butler desired to destroy. On May 7th Beauregard reached Petersburg, Va., with his army, and Butler, finding his movement towards Richmond endangered by the presence of Beauregard in his flank and rear, withdrew his army inside his fortifications at Bermuda Hundred, determined to direct his operations against Petersburg. General Grant, however, ordered the larger portion of his force to the assistance of the Army of the Potomac, and Butler gave up his place and joined Grant on the Chickahominy.—From a sketch by E. F. Mullen.

RESCUING THE SURVIVORS

THE "WEEHAWKEN'S" GRAVE.

THE "WEEHAWKEN" SINKING, DEC 1ᵗ 1863

SINKING OF THE MONITOR "WEEHAWKEN" DURING THE SIEGE OF CHARLESTON, S. C.—On December 6, 1863, the monitor "Wehawken," which had taken an active part in the siege of Charleston, and had received and resisted on her turret and deck over one hundred solid shot from Fort Sumter and the neighboring batteries, was moored off Morris Island, having just received a heavy weight of ammunition for another attack. Owing to bad trim a large volume of water was admitted through the ports and under the turret, which carried her down so rapidly that four officers and twenty of her crew were lost before assistance could reach the vessel.—From sketches by W. T. Crane.

221

PRESENTATION OF COLORS TO THE TWENTIETH UNITED STATES COLORED INFANTRY, Colonel Bertram, in Union Square, New York city, March 5, 1864.—This illustration, as sketched by the artist, is of a scene that was unique in the experience of the "looker-on" in New York even in war times. In a city where but a few years before an occasional street car had displayed the legend "Colored Persons Allowed to Ride in this Car," and where only two years before negroes had been hung on the lamp-posts of the public streets by a riotous mob, now an entire regiment of colored soldiers, armed and equipped by the Federal Government, were presented with colors and cheered to the echo as they departed to take part in the defense of their Government.—From a sketch by A. Berghaus.

NEW YEAR'S CONTRABAND BALL AT VICKSBURG, MISS., DURING THE SIEGE.—Mr. Schell did not confine the work of his pencil to "war scenes," but caught as well the spirit of frolic so irrepressible in the negro. While the anxiety of the white inhabitants of the beleaguered city prevented any frivolity, and they were spending their Christmas holidays in fear and apprehension of their fate, the negro, forgetful of aught but the passing of another Christmas-tide and its attendant festivities, determined to round out the season by a dance, accompanied by song to the tune of the banjo and fiddle, from which the negro melodies float in ever-increasing volume and time, until the very floor groans beneath the tread of the incessant "heel and toe," and the singers almost raise the roof with the volume of their notes.—From a sketch by **F. B. Schell**.

Bombardment of Fort Moultrie.

BOMBARDMENT OF FORT MOULTRIE AND BATTERIES BEE AND BEAUREGARD, CHARLESTON HARBOR, S. C., SEPTEMBER 5, 6, 1863.
INTERIOR OF BATTERY GREGG, LOOKING TOWARDS FORT WAGNER.—The Federal fleet of ironclads on September 5th opened a forty-two-hour bombardment on Fort Moultrie, on Sullivan Island, and Batteries Bee and Beauregard, which were smaller batteries on either side of the fort. Late on the 6th General Gillman was ready for an assault on Fort Wagner, on Morris Island, that he had planned and prepared from his position on the lower portion of the island, his sappers having already mined the counterscarp of Fort Wagner. On the morning of the 7th his pickets leading the assaulting party found the fort evacuated, as well as Battery Gregg, on the extreme northern extremity of the island. These forts were immediately enlarged and strengthened, and as they commanded Fort Sumter as well as the city of Charleston, the heavy guns of Gillman effectually shelled both the fort and the city.—From sketches by W. T. Crane.

BATTLE OF JAMES' ISLAND, S. C.—Bayonet charge of the Federal troops, under General Stevens, upon the Confederate batteries. The Confederate force, under Colonel Lamar, held possession of a powerful earthwork, which proved troublesome, as it was out of range of the guns of the Federal vessels. It was protected by a well-constructed abattis, and was so stubbornly defended that it was captured only after an attack in force, during which the Federal troops made one of the most brilliant charges of the war. In the face of a galling fire the Federals advanced, tore through the obstructions and carried the place at the point of the bayonet.—Sketched by an Officer.

BATTLE OF SAVAGE'S STATION.—Smith's division in action. "Stonewall" Jackson brought from the Shenandoah Valley into Ashland his army of 35,000 men. The approach of Jackson and an intended attack by General Lee were known to the Federals, and preparations were made to repulse the attack. McClellan, learning that Lee was directing the movement, concluded to fall back toward the James River. The stores were ordered to be removed to Savage Station, where he also sent the wounded. On the 28th Ewell's division with the Confederate cavalry, crossed the river and attacked in force. General Smith's division made a brave stand and attempted to stem the advance, but, owing to the superior number, was forced to retire. McClellan then ordered the abandonment of all the Federal works at Savage's Station and retreated to a new base on the James River.—Sketched by William Waud.

BATTLE OF SLAUGHTER'S MOUNTAIN.—General Pope concentrated his army near Culpepper Court House. A reconnoitering party occupied Orange Court House. Seeing this, Jackson and Ewell crossed the Rapidan and advanced upon Slaughter's Mountain, where Banks and Crawford were stationed. Ewell was ordered to the west of the mountain, while Early formed a line of battle upon the ridge on the right. Banks was taken at a disadvantage, for he had not only a superior force to contend with, but the Confederates were stationed upon an elevation from which their batteries were very effective. He advanced at once across the fields under a perfect storm of shot and shell until he reached the base of the mountain, when a Confederate force emerged from the works and compelled a retreat. They were relentlessly pursued until they reached the line which Pope had formed with Rickett's division of McDowell's corps.—Sketched by Edwin Forbes.

BATTLE OF THE CHICKAHOMINY.—McClellan facing the forces of Lee and Jackson. On the 26th of June, 1862, the Confederates began an advance against the Federal line. Meeting with but little opposition, Hill pushed on to Beaver Dam Creek, unsuspicious that 5,000 men and batteries were on the heights overlooking the creek, waiting for his coming, with'n easy range of musketry to give him a warm welcome. In spite of the infantry and artillery poured into them the Confederates pushed to the creek, but were unable to cross. They then directed their attention to the right and left of the line, but were badly repulsed, and at nine o'clock in the evening they retired.—Sketched by William Waud.

BOMBARDMENT OF ISLAND NO. 10 AND THE CONFEDERATE FORTIFICATION OF THE KENTUCKY SHORE.—General Halleck desired to clear the Mississippi River, and sent Commodore Foote with a fleet, which was joined at Columbus by two regiments of infantry. This force anchored five miles above the island. They found the place almost impregnable to assault by one series of batteries above another, in all of which were mounted guns of the heaviest calibre. The bombardment began on the 16th of March, and was kept up incessantly all the afternoon without eliciting a response, and without apparently causing any damage. The Federals lashed together three of their gunboats and made a somewhat novel and formidable floating battery, and with this they dismounted a few of the enemy's guns.—Sketched by H. Lovie.

NIGHT ATTACK ON ISLAND NO. 10.—The day after the bombardment described on the preceding page and all through the following night the mortar boats continued throwing shells. They were reinforced in the morning by six additional boats sent from Cairo. The firing was continued with hardly an intermission for three days, and finally succeeded in silencing the upper Confederate battery on the Kentucky shore. The mortar boats continued the firing for about a week, when it was found to be impossible to take the place by the fleet alone, and it was decided to send a land force.—Sketched by Henry Lovie.

THE NAVAL BATTLE IN HAMPTON ROADS between the Confederate vessels "Merrimac," "Yorktown" and "Jamestown," and the Federal frigates "Cumberland" and "Congress."—Sinking of the "Cumberland," and victory of the Confederate navy, March 8, 1862. It had long been known that the Confederates were fashioning a formidable engine of war, and it now appeared in the shape of a huge floating battery, carrying eight eighty-pound rifled guns. This was the "Merrimac;" she attacked the "Cumberland," pouring in broadside after broadside, and then retiring for a distance under full steam drove her ram into the side of the "Cumberland," sinking her in a few moments. She then engaged the water battery, shelled the Federal camp, and afterwards poured such a broadside into the "Congress" as to compel her to surrender. While this was going on the other Federal vessels were ordered forward.—Sketched by W. T. Crane.

FIGHT BETWEEN THE "MONITOR" AND THE "MERRIMAC."—The conflict described on the preceding page caused great anxiety as to the future, when Ericsson's floating battery was seen approaching Fortress Monroe. This was the "Monitor," whose deck lay but a few inches above the water and had nothing but a round revolving tower, twenty feet in diameter, in which were two eleven-inch Dahlgren guns. On the 9th of March the "Merrimac" again appeared and advanced against the "Minnesota," but the "Monitor" intercepted her, and both began a rapid interchange of shots. The fight continued for two hours, the "Monitor" having her turret penetrated halfway by a one-hundred-pound shot, and pouring her heavy bolts against the "Merrimac" without doing any apparent damage. Not succeeding in damaging the "Monitor," the "Merrimac" turned her attention to the "Minnesota," which had grounded, but the "Monitor" renewed her attack, and drove her back to Norfolk.—Sketched by W. T. Crane.

GENERAL ROSECRANS AND HIS STAFF at their headquarters, Clarksburg, Va., while commanding the Department of Western Virginia.   General Rosecrans, who since he succeeded General McClellan on July 22, 1861, had been organizing a large army, learned early in the month of September that the Confederates forces, under General Floyd, were at Carnifax Court House.   Rosecrans determined to attack Floyd without delay, before the Confederate became in a still better position to menace the Federals in Western Virginia, and took command of the forces in person.—Sketched by F. B. Schell.

SUNKEN HULKS AT THE MOUTH OF THE SAVANNAH RIVER.—In the expedition against Port Royal, Commodore Dupont of the Federal fleet found almost every Southern harbor blocked by sunken vessels, which greatly delayed operations. The fleet consisted of sixteen ships, besides twenty-three transports and other sailing vessels. The land forces were under command of General Sherman.

SKIRMISH NEAR BEAUFORT, S. C., between Confederate cavalry and the Federal pickets.—On the 9th of November the city of Beaufort was captured and its arsenal destroyed.—Sketched by W. T. Crane.

234

SCENE IN THE MILITARY MARKET AT BEAUFORT, S. C.—The reoccupation of South Carolina was the cause of great rejoicing throughout the North, and celebrations were rendered more extensive when the Secretaries of the Army and Navy by general order directed that a salute be fired from each navy yard in honor of the event. Expeditions were sent out to take possession of all the neighboring positions which could be utilized in the future for defense or offense, and they were either demolished or fortified and manned with Federal troops. Beaufort remained the base of supplies, and its market was an interesting and busy scene.—Sketched by W. T. Crane.

BURNSIDE'S ARMY CROSSING THE RAPPAHANNOCK RIVER.—Upon assuming command. Burnside reorganized his forces with a view to an early campaign against Richmond and began a forward movement on the 15th November, 1862, against Fredericksburg; his advance was spread out on the north side of the Rappahannock and began to cross on the 10th of December, over five pontoon bridges protected by 29 batteries of 147 guns. The Confederates opened fire and frustrated the attempt, when Burnside opened fire upon the city and set it on fire in several places. Under cover of the night General Hooker's division crossed and preparations were completed for an assault in the morning.— Sketched by Henry Lovie.

TEH NEW GENERAL HOSPITAL HILTON HEAD S.C.

U. S. HOSPITAL AT HILTON HEAD.—In May, 1862, the Federals were in entire possession of the Atlantic coast with the exception of Charleston.   Various expeditions, under different commanders, were made during the remainder of the year, but without leading to any result.   The forces rested at Hilton Head, where a large hospital was erected.—Sketched by W. T. Crane.

EXTEMPORE ENTERTAINMENT OF THE TROOPS.—During the occupation of Baton Rouge the troops gave themselves up to whatever amusement could be found. There was an increasing interest in the colored people, who were always happy and care-free under all circumstances. The illustration shows a musical and terpischorean entertainment at the U. S. Arsenal, under the patronage of the Forty-first Massachusetts, the One-hundred and Thirty-first New York and the Thirty-fourth Connecticut Volunteers.—Sketched by F. B. Schell.

LIBBY PRISON, RICHMOND, VA.—This notorious prison was built for a tobacco warehouse, and consisted of five lofts and a cellar. The building stood upon a hill which descended abruptly to the canal, from which its southern wall was only divided by a street. It was entirely detached, making it a comparatively easy matter to guard those confined within by a small force, and keep every door and window in full view. There were nine large rooms, 45 x 105, with eight feet from floor to ceiling, except on the upper floor, which was higher, owing to the pitch of the roof. In these rooms the prisoners were crowded by hundreds. The basement, called the "rat-hole," was not occupied, as there the men would be out of sight. A party of 109 prisoners, headed by Capt. T. E. Rose, escaped by boring a tunnel from this cellar to a vacant lot. Of the whole number who escaped only 59 after incredible hardships reached the Federal lines. This was one of the most remarkable escapes known to history.—Sketched by Theodore R. Davis.

RECAPTURE OF A TRAIN FROM MOSEBY'S GUERILLAS.—Col. John S. Moseby commanded a body of horse and made incursions into the Federal lines, and at one time penetrated as far as Fairfax Court House, retiring thence only after he had effected the capture of Colonel Shoughton and a large part of his brigade, besides destroying and carrying away a large amount of valuable property. The illustration represents an attack upon Moseby while carrying off a train, and its recapture by the Federals.—Sketched by Edwin Forbes.

EXTERIOR VIEW OF FORTIFICATIONS AT HILTON HEAD.—The Federals desired a place of rendezvous in the South and sent a powerful naval and military force to Port Royal, which captured the fort at Hilton Head. General Sherman set about fortifying the forts at Hilton Head and Bay Point, Fort Walker being named Fort Welles, and Fort Beauregard named Fort Seward, while Commodore Dupont organized armed expeditions throughout the islands, which proved everywhere successful.—Sketched by W. T. Crane.

INTERIOR OF MORTAR BATTERY, TYBEE ISLAND.—After the occupation of Hilton Head Island an expedition was sent to take possession of Tybee Island, at the entrance of the Savannah River. Mortar Batteries were erected on the island, and on the 10th of April Fort Pulaski was bombarded.   The illustration shows the operation of the 13-inch mortar during the bombardment.—Sketched by W. T. Crane.

PANORAMIC VIEW OF CHARLESTON HARBOR.—1. The attack of the ironclads.   2. Night after the fight; the ironclads at anchor off Fort Sumter.— Sketched by W. T. Crane.

243

THE FUNERAL CORTEGE OF THE SOLDIERS KILLED AT BALTIMORE PASSING THE BOSTON COMMON.—The bodies were received in Boston by a military escort under Governor Andrew, accompanied by a large concourse of people. All the mills and stores were closed and all business suspended. The funeral services were held in Huntingdon Hall, and the bodies deposited in a vault of the Lowell Cemetery.

"BILLY" WILSON'S ZOUAVES TAKING THE OATH.—This was the Sixth New York Regiment, which was recruited from the rowdy and criminal element of New York City. Colonel Wilson mustered his regiment in Tammany Hall, and with a sword in one hand and the American flag in the other, knelt on one knee, the entire regiment doing the same, and swore to support the flag.

DEPARTURE OF TROOPS AND MUNITIONS OF WAR FROM COLLINS LINE DOCK, NEW YORK CITY.—Between the 15th of April and the 1st of May, 1861, $40,000,000 was voluntarily contributed for war purposes by the Northern States. By the end of 1861 the State of New York had one hundred and seven volunteer regiments in the field.

SHIPMENTS OF WAR MATERIAL FROM NEW YORK.—The uprising of the people was immediate; within fifteen days from the 15th of April 350,000 troops were mustered from the North and West. Every State contributed four to ten times the quota asked for. Pennsylvania troops were the first to reach Washington.

REVIEW OF THE CLINCH RIFLES on the parade ground of the United States Arsenal at Augusta, Ga., February, 1861.—From the date of Georgia's secession Governor Brown with characteristic promptitude hastened to make practical the sovereignty of the State.   He demanded the surrender of the arsenal at Augusta, which was agreed upon by Captain Elzey on the 24th of January, 1861, when the Clinch Rifles, a State militia organization, took possession in the name of the State of Georgia.—Sketched by a Southern Officer.

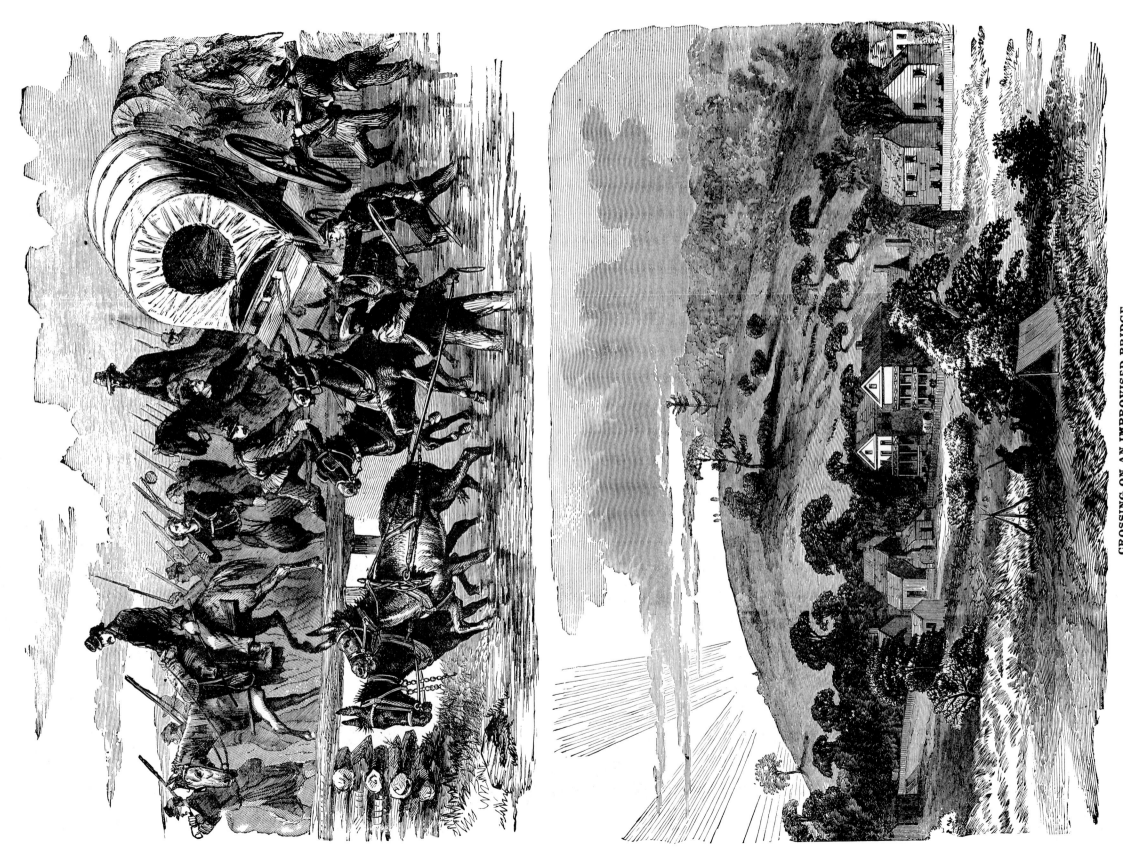

CROSSING ON AN IMPROVISED BRIDGE.

ALDIE, THE SCENE OF GENERAL PLEASANTON'S VICTORIOUS CAVALRY ENGAGEMENT.—A reconnoissance in force toward Culpepper Court House was ordered by General Pleasanton, which resulted in a severe battle at Aldie with Stuart's forces.—Sketched by Edwin Forbes.

249

SEIZURE OF THE UNITED STATES ARSENAL AT CHARLESTON, S. C.—The United States held possession of the Arsenal in Charleston and of Fort Sumter, which had been ceded to the United States to be held for the protection of Charleston and harbor. Governor Pickens took possession of the Arsenal and demanded the surrender of Fort Sumter.—Sketched by a Southern Officer.

DESTRUCTION OF THE "MERRIMAC."—The Confederate ironclad was blown up by her commander, May 11th, 1862, after the destruction of Norfolk Navy Yard.

LOSS OF THE MONITOR IN A STORM OFF CAPE HATTERAS, DECEMBER 30, 1862.—Gallant effort to rescue her crew by the "Rhode Island."

FLANK MOVEMENT UPON THE CONFEDERATE WORKS.—In the operations before Petersburgh the Second Corps crossed to the west side of Thatcher's Run by a swinging movement to seize the Southside railroad.

NORTHERN MEN PROCURING NEGRO SUBSTITUTES.

GRAND REVIEW OF THE UNITED STATES ARMY AT WASHINGTON, D. C., MAY 23, 1865.—Troops marching up Pennsylvania avenue before passing the reviewing stand.—This was one of the greatest military pageants ever seen. The armies of Grant and Sherman, as they passed through Washington, were marshaled in review. Over 200,000 troops were assembled in one body for the first time, gathered from every battlefield of the war. The returning soldiers, as they passed through the streets, were welcomed with grateful shouts. Their banners were torn, their arms and dress were battle-soiled, and many an absent one was mourned; but they had served their country, and their step was proud and triumphant.—Sketched by W. T. Crane.

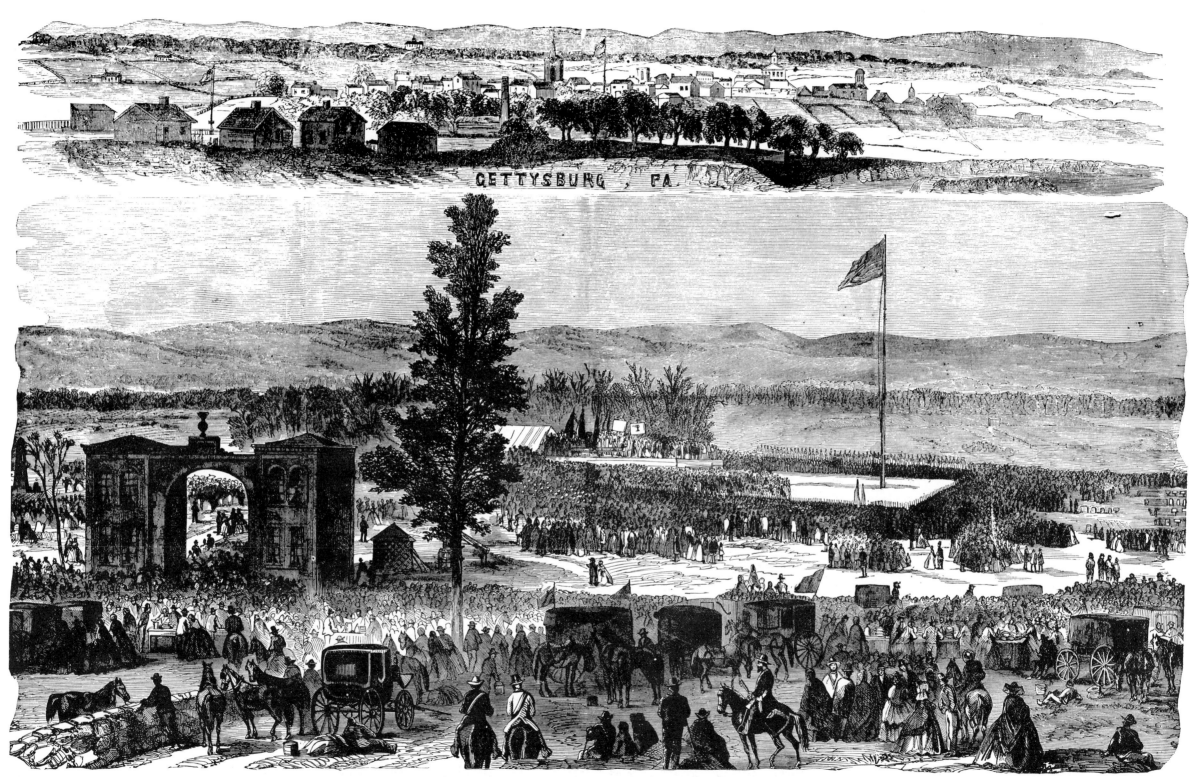

GETTYSBURG, PA.

CONSECRATION OF THE NATIONAL CEMETERY AT GETTYSBURG, NOV. 18, 1863, BY ABRAHAM LINCOLN, PRESIDENT OF THE UNITED STATES.—He delivered a speech which was at once recognized as the philosophy of the whole great struggle in brief which has become classic in the language. His closing words were: "We cannot hallow this ground, the brave men living and dead who struggled here have consecrated it far above our power to add or detract. It is rather for us to be here dedicated to the great task remaining before us, that we here highly resolve that these dead shall not have died in vain—that this nation under God shall have a new birth of freedom—and that government of the people by the people for the people shall not perish from the earth.—Sketched by Joseph Becker.

ON FAME'S ETERNAL CAMPING GROUND
THEIR SILENT TENTS ARE SPREAD
AND GLORY GUARDS WITH SOLEMN ROUND
THE BIVOAC OF THE DEAD.

REVISITING THE BATTLEFIELDS OF VIRGINIA.—On Thursday, the 15th of May, 1884, the veterans of the Army of the Potomac together with a large party of distinguished persons assembled at Fredericksburg for the purpose of visiting the battlefields of Virginia. The group under the umbrella are Major Stein, General Longstreet and General Rosecrans examining the plan of the battle of Fredericksburg. General Doubleday explained the movements and positions of the Federal line at the battle of Fredericksburg. Colonel Oats of Alabama pointed out the Confederate position. General Ayres and Mr. C. C. Coffin described the movements of the artillery. They visited Chancellorsville, Spottsylvania Court House and other chief points of interest.

DECORATION DAY.—Memorial Day was first instituted by John A. Logan, comrade of the Grand Army of the Republic, and on the 30th of May each year has been proudly observed. It has become a national holiday, and means to perpetuate, by floral offerings and orations in commemoration of the dead, the memory of those only who wore the Union blue and fought in defense of the flag of our common country. The foundation of the Grand Army of the Republic was laid by Dr. B. F. Stephenson, of Springfield, Ill. He had thought deeply upon the best way to band together after the war the men who wore the blue, and by degrees during the war perfected his plan. Representative soldiers were called together at Springfield, July 12, 1866, and duly mustered in and given authority to organize posts in their respective towns. Gen. John M. Palmer was made chief officer. Departments were immediately organized in all the States, until its membership now numbers over a quarter of a million.